DON'T
PANIC

Daily Mirror

No. 11,040. ONE PENNY

Registered at the G.P.O. as a Newspaper
Geraldine House, Fetter-lane, E.C.4.
HOLBORN 4321

CONSCRIPTION— ALL MEN 18-21 MUST BE SOLDIERS

ALL PAY Budget

SIR JOHN SIMON'S peace-time war Budget of £942,600,000 was favourably received in the House of Commons, the City and throughout the country last night.

Socialists in the House of Commons generally approved, and a millionaire M.P., who will be hit by the surtax increases, commented: "It is hard, but fair."

Chief points—the Chancellor announced are:—

There is no increase in income tax.

Tax on private cars is raised from 15s. to 25s. per horse-power as from next January 1. Motor-cycle taxes will be raised correspondingly.

Sugar duty raised by ¼d. per lb. from five o'clock last night.

Tobacco duty up by 2s. per lb. This increase will be passed on to smokers. It is approximately 1¼d. an ounce, and cigarette smokers will probably pay the same price for a packet of fewer cigarettes.

This arrangement would not interfere with the automatic machine trade.

Surtax is increased. Incomes from £2,000 to £8,000 will be taxed a further 5 per cent., and incomes above £8,000 a further 10 per cent.

Death duties go up. Estates of over £50,000 will pay an additional 10 per cent. There is no tax increase on agricultural property.

Photographic films and plates will be taxed. The rate is to be about 2d. on the popular sizes of roll films.

Theatres Gain

And Sir John Simon announced two concessions to the taxpayer.

Entertainments tax on the "living theatre" is reduced so as to cut prices by 1d. This will operate from September 3 next.

Medicine stamp duties are repealed. The duties were, said Sir John, "a troublesome question which I propose to settle once and for all." The medicine tax had brought in a revenue of £590,000.

A new drive is to be launched on the tax-dodger. It will be directed, the Chancellor declared, "against the ingenious use of the one-man company."

The Budget has been framed, Sir John stressed, to meet the "cruel necessity" of leaping defence costs.

In the coming year £630,000,000 will be spent on defence instead of the £580,000,000 he estimated only two months ago.

"And," Sir John Simon added ominously, "it may well be more."

Defence £13 a Head

The Chancellor in a broadcast speech last night said:—

"No one will escape.

"The five tax increases—motor-cars, surtax, estate duty, tobacco and sugar—have been arranged to call for a contribution from all kinds of citizens.

"I am well assured that British citizens are willing to do all that is needed to make Britain safe and strong and free.

"Our defence expenditure this year—£630,000,000 was not far short of £2,000,000 a day. It was £13 per head of the population of the United Kingdom. It was more than three times the total public expenditure for all purposes before the war.

"Though these burdens are hard to bear," Sir John added, "remember that in these difficult days Britain's best contribution to the peace of the world is that she herself should be strong."

Budget Speech—Page 24.
W. M. on the Budget—Page 13.

30 FEET

A baby fell 30ft. from the open window you see in this picture . . . he was caught by the shop sun blind and suffered nothing worse than a bruised nose.

You'll find his picture—and the full story—on page 3.

34 Millions a Year More

Total estimated effect of the alterations proposed in the Budget are £24,270,000 increase this year and £33,945,000 in a full year.

The principal receipts are estimated at:
Income tax, £327,000,000.
Surtax, £76,000,000.
Estate duties, £89,000,000.
Stamps, £21,000,000.
National Defence Contribution, £25,000,000.
Other inland revenue duties, £1,250,000.
Total inland revenue, £534,250,000.
Customs and Excise, £349,020,000.
Motor vehicle duties, £43,450,000.
Total receipts from taxes, £916,720,000.
Total revenue, £942,690,000.

AFTER A DRAMATIC CABINET MEETING LAST NIGHT —THE FIRST EVER KNOWN TO BE CALLED IMME-DIATELY AFTER A BUDGET SPEECH — THE GOVERN-MENT DECIDED TO INTRODUCE A SCHEME OF COMPUL-SORY MILITARY TRAINING.

Mr. Chamberlain later paid a surprise visit to the King at Buckingham Palace, and informed him of the vital decision taken. He remained with the King for nearly an hour.

In the House of Commons to-day the Premier will announce the Cabinet's plan, and a Bill will later be introduced to make the scheme law.

The Government have decided, says the "Daily Mirror" Political Correspondent, to conscript men between the ages of eighteen and twenty-one—it may be raised to twenty-three—for a short period of military training.

Soldiers thus enrolled will follow their compulsory service with a short period in the Territorial Army.

Million Men

There are available over a million men between the ages of eighteen and twenty-one. Many are in reserved occupations and the reserved list is likely to be revised to free the greatest possible number of men.

If the age limit is raised to twenty-five over 3,000,000 men would be available—too many for the Army to train in the immediate future.

Two main reasons have influenced the Government in coming to a conscription decision:

(1) Pressure from France, Poland, Rumania and Greece for a sign of Britain's capacity to fulfil her pledges.

(2) Representations from the Army Council, who consider that conscription is imperative if full advantage is to be taken of our defence resources.

By Age Classes

The Government will not attempt to force the Conscription Bill through the House. They will welcome long debates in the knowledge that in view of facts regarding the international situation the country will realise the need for immediate conscription.

The scheme will be so arranged as to provide the maximum number of instructors for the period of service.

It is proposed to conscript men by age classes. The Government are prepared to make concessions to the Labour and Trade Union movements in order to remove their opposition.

Mr. Chamberlain will see Labour and Trade Union delegates this morning before he makes his statement in the House of Commons.

A special Cabinet committee will consider Trade Union objections to compulsion. These objections have already been submitted to the Premier.

In order to placate the Labour movement, Mr. Chamberlain is likely to offer a capital levy—a tax on all capital.

He will also give a pledge in regard to dilution of unskilled labour in arms factories.

WHICH?
QUAKER WHEAT or QUAKER RICE?

QUAKER RICE

YOU choose *Shirley Temple's* breakfast!

QUAKER WHEAT

Star of "Just around the corner" a 20th-Century Fox Picture

New breakfast-time game! Choose Shirley Temple's breakfast for her. She said "Quaker Wheat's *my* cereal"—then she tried Quaker Rice, and she quickly added "I love Quaker Rice, too!"

Now—which is it to be? Quaker Wheat comes in delicious crisp golden grains! Quaker Rice snowy white—quite a new breakfast flavour.

Both Quaker Wheat and Quaker Rice are "shot from guns"—exploded to eight times normal size, so that its energy is easily used. Both Quaker Wheat and Quaker Rice are ready to eat. So simple to serve, too—just lift the patent flap and pour.

Get a packet of each today—and choose Shirley Temple's breakfast for her tomorrow!

QUAKER WHEAT—QUAKER RICE

DON'T PANIC

Britain Prepares
for Invasion, 1940

MARK ROWE

SPELLMOUNT

First published 2010

The History Press
The Mill, Brimscombe Port
Stroud, Gloucestershire, GL5 2QG
www.thehistorypress.co.uk

British Library Cataloguing in Publication Data.
A catalogue record for this book is available from the British Library.

ISBN 978 0 7524 5609 6

Typesetting and origination by The History Press
Printed in India by Replika Press Pvt. Ltd.
Manufacturing managed by Jellyfish Print Solutions Ltd

CONTENTS

CHAPTER 1

THE FIRST SHOCK: PARATROOPERS

'We're here because we're here because we're here because we're here.'
(A soldier's lament sung to the tune of 'Auld Lang Syne')

Sir George Schuster was the sort of man who knew if you were going wrong; and he would tell you so. In a letter – a long letter – printed in *The Times* on Friday 10 May 1940, he called for national unity; and what he called a 'national government'. As the National Liberal MP for Walsall, he was calling, in political code, for an end to Conservative Neville Chamberlain's government. By the time the letter was in print, Winston Churchill was Prime Minister. That morning, Germany attacked France, Belgium and the Netherlands. Sir George had new telephone calls to make, letters to write and tempests to call up.

Walsall Mayor J. Cliff Tibbits sent a letter to Sir George's central London home on Monday 13 May. Tibbits recalled a weekend letter and telephone call from Sir George. The Mayor had spoken with the local Chief Constable, who saw Sir George's letter. All agreed: *something should be done*. Tibbits wrote:

He [the Chief Constable] is confident that a strong force can be recruited if called immediately. Arms would of course have to be provided. The Chief Constable agrees with me that Walsall's aerodrome is a weak spot in the district and we should like a military guard on the site of the aerodrome. The aerodrome is only a small one but any troops landed there can be in New Street, Birmingham in 15 minutes. I have also been concerned about the protection of the Generating Stations of the West Midland Electricity Authority … As far as I know the police are not armed and they have been doing all they can for six months so it hardly seems possible that they can now increase their efforts.

Royal Engineers pose in front of a sandbagged machine-gun post at Admiralty Arch in London. (War Office official photograph, May 1940)

Sir George wrote back to Tibbits on Thursday 16 May. He had been trying to find out more about local defence schemes – the typed word 'schemes' was crossed out and 'volunteers' written above. 'All that the War Office could tell him was that 'full particulars will be published in the next day or two.' Sir George felt strongly that the Mayor should satisfy himself about 'who is concerting measures':

> Everyone now seems to be devoting attention to the matter of raising a new corps but it seems to me that that must be a secondary consideration and what I should want to know is not how new men are to be raised but how such forces as are already available are going to be used to protect the essential points. I asked the War Office who the area commander was in your case and all they could say was that you would be able to find this out in the telephone book. From what you told me before, the regional commissioner's office in your case seems to take the line that it is not their business, but I understand that they definitely are concerned and again if I were in your place I would get on to them … I am not at all satisfied as to the way in which these things are being done and indeed all these schemes ought to have been worked out long ago … It seems to me however that the only thing to do now in order to ensure that proper arrangements are being made is for people on the spot in each area to worry the authorities and find out what the arrangements are.

Such was the beginning of Britain's finest hour, as defined by Churchill and echoed by all ever since. It started on 10 May with the German invasion of Western Europe, quickly and shockingly successful, ending in winter when the threat of a German invasion of Britain went away until the spring. All the ingredients of the summer were in Sir George's flurry of letters: exaggerated yet vivid fears for the worst – Germans landing at Walsall's grass airfield and driving stolen cars nine miles to Birmingham city centre in a quarter of an hour; critics 'worrying' the authorities with their bright ideas; and those in authority confused by that frightening and thankfully rare phenomenon in life, something important and unavoidable. Britain faced the greatest risk of invasion since Napoleon.

SHOOT FIRST – BUT WITH WHAT?

The sudden, novel and real threat of paratroopers making Britain their next stop after Belgium and Holland brought out the genuinely patriotic, the know-alls, and madmen who liked to write to newspapers and see their names in print.

E.R. Lansdale, of Petersfinger, near Salisbury, was a former soldier. He was 'Giggleswick School OTC 1920–4', according to the letter he wrote to Southern Command headquarters in Salisbury on 13 May. He was careful to put on paper all his military experience – that he had helped run a school's officer training corps – because he was asking for his name to go on the waiting list 'if it were decided to issue rifles to householders on the outskirts of towns and having a good field of fire and who are accustomed to the use of service rifles'. Lansdale included – and the Army filed it, so that today it sits in the National Archives – a clipping from the previous day's *Sunday Express*. According to the newspaper,

> … it would be a wise precaution to issue free arms licences and permits to buy ammunition to men possessing revolvers, rifles or guns who are judged trustworthy by police. There are enough such persons all over the country to deal with isolated raiders. It would be well to inform the public that the parachutist is trained in every sort of trick. Anyone taken in by a friendly gesture or a sign of surrender will certainly be shot. Shoot first is the only safe motto; in any case parachute troops are a form of warfare that should be discouraged.

The same day, a Major W.A.D. Edwardes sent a reply to Lansdale, ending: 'Meanwhile should you spot any parachutists doubtless you will take such steps as you would take to be necessary in the national interest.' As yet the Army had no authority to form 'contra-parachutists groups'.

It is significant that Mr Lansdale enclosed the newspaper cutting, drawing support for his fears, and for presuming to write to the Army, from what he read.

War Office official photograph, May 1940. Grenadier Guards making sandbag defences around government buildings in Birdcage Walk, London, in response to fears of parachutist attacks.

Barbed wire and sandbag defences being built outside government buildings on the corner of Horse Guards Road, Great George Street and Birdcage Walk, London. (War Office official photograph, May 1940)

Around the country, newspapers fed quite suddenly fears of a new kind of warfare, fears that for a few days the government could not calm.

The Tuesday evening after the Friday shock of the German attack, the new Secretary of State for War, Anthony Eden, went on the radio to announce what soon became the LDV – Local Defence Volunteers. What happened in between? Plenty of talking. At 3pm on Saturday 11 May a meeting at the Home Office

Above: New Street, Birmingham. Walsall MP Sir George Schuster worried in a private letter in May 1940 that German invaders to his constituency might steal lorries, head for the city centre, and paralyse it.

Left: Anthony Eden, who broadcast for defence volunteers on 14 May 1940.

discussed arming the police. The Metropolitan Police Commissioner Sir Philip Game strongly opposed any arming of his police. As for police on guard at factories, telephone exchanges, and so on, chief constables could arm their men if necessary, the meeting heard. The job of police on patrol was to watch, and even if they were armed they could only deal with two or three saboteurs or parachutists. The meeting agreed chief constables could still use their discretion. In any case, the police had fairly few weapons in stock: 1,000 rifles, mainly around the coasts, 5,000 revolvers and 3,000 automatics. Even if the police took up arms, it was doubtful whether as many men were trained in their use as the number of firearms to hand.

A secret 12 May memo went from the Home Office to chief constables. It called for a state of 'maximum efficiency' for dealing with the possibility of enemy landing by parachute. Speed was of utmost importance; if police saw an invader they should report at once to the nearest Army or Royal Air Force station. As for the public sighting 'any persons landing by parachute', the memo admitted: 'It is inevitable that a large proportion of these reports should be unfounded and the police will no doubt do everything possible to verify their accuracy; this should not however delay the communication of the information to the military authorities.' And as for arming of the police, it was 'reasonable that police guarding important vulnerable points particularly in the southern and south-eastern part of the country should be armed with revolvers on a more general scale than has hitherto been the case.' But there was no general issue of arms. So the government stressed that if anyone saw paratroopers, they should tell the authorities. Sensible, even obvious advice: but then what?

WISE BEFORE THE EVENT

Meanwhile, ordinary people were having the same ideas. G.H. Cookes, secretary of the Nuneaton branch of the British Legion, told his local weekly newspaper:

> Before Mr Eden had made his appeal for volunteers two of our members came to see me to see whether we could do something as a branch to take a lead. I got in touch with one or two people and went to see Supt Cresswell [the local police chief] who was very pleased to see us.

Even quicker off the mark was someone who signed themselves 'Prepared', who had a letter printed in Sir George Schuster's constituency newspaper, the *Walsall Observer & South Staffordshire Chronicle*, on 11 May 1940. 'Prepared' proposed a volunteer defence corps, under former officers and non-commissioned officers.

> This corps should be trained for use in the event of enemy action in this country, to be ready to meet any surprise landing of troops by enemy planes … available day and night to deal with any such opposition until such time as detachments of regular troops could reach the place.

This is close to a description of what became the Home Guard.

When the war was over, understandably some people claimed that they had the idea first. Major John Maxse, in an undated memo after the war for the War Office, went over the claims. Maxse's yardstick: did a claimant put it in words as used by Eden in his crucial 14 May 1940 broadcast? What Eden had said was based on words by the Commander in Chief Home Forces, General Sir Walter Kirke, and chief of staff Brigadier W. Carden Roe, and the adjutant general, General Sir Robert Gordon-Finlayson.

Despite the raising of battalions for home defence, in the months between the start of war in September 1939 and May 1940, Britain became if anything shorter of soldiers. Before and after the Germans invaded Denmark in April, the British authorities agreed that the best insurance against an invasion of Britain was to send front-line soldiers, the British Expeditionary Force (BEF), to France, and 'less advanced formations', too, who could better finish their training nearer the front line.

In Britain, even before 10 May, everyone in authority at strategic locations – ports, gasworks, factories, airfields – wanted guards. In Maxse's words 'penny packets', little groups of soldiers on guard dotted over the country, threatened to deprive Kirke of any concentrated mobile reserve to deal with parachutists, the only danger in those days. Kirke felt the need for a home defence force like the First World War Volunteer Force. The Army Council in a letter of 7 May 1940 to Home Commands in Britain's regions said it was considering a Volunteer Home

Army. In other words, when talking among themselves the generals and the government saw the need for home guards, but only when the Germans got too close for comfort did they act on it.

Events moved fast – so fast that it's easy to miss the stages of the rising threat. In the first days after 10 May a few voices recalled that the country had gone through it all before, during the First World War. The *Derbyshire Times* in its editorial of 17 May 1940, the Friday after Eden's appeal for LDVs on the Tuesday evening, noted:

> In the last war the Home Guards were a valuable adjunct to home defence and there is no reason why the new defence body should not be more useful with enlarged activities especially if they are quickly trained to shoot. This is where the British Legion of ex-servicemen and men who can handle firearms can form a valuable nucleus.

THE EXAMPLE OF 1914–18 AND EARLIER

Continent-facing counties had done most to prepare in case of invasion in the First World War. In Norfolk, for example, the authorities had grappled with questions that cropped up again in 1940: should cattle be shot rather than fall into enemy hands? Should cattle or fleeing people be allowed to get in the way of troops on the roads? Would Norwich, on the likely route of an invader, be defended? (The view in 1915 was that it would not.)

Some people remembered how it had been the last time around. The *Bromsgrove Weekly Messenger*, for instance, opined on 18 May:

> The formation of this LDV is a step similar to that taken in the last war, when those whose duty lay at home evinced a spontaneous desire to help the country in a more active way than merely carrying on civilian pursuits. The Volunteers were armed and equipped and grouped in battalions and were assigned special tasks including a mobile cycle corps that patrolled the East Coast to watch for possible invaders.

Some had more vivid recollections; 'Mr Leicester' in a regular column in the *Leicester Mercury* on 24 May harked back to a citizens defence corps training camp at nearby Syston, under canvas, and how he slept in a blanket on the ground.

Those 1914 volunteer home defence forces sprang up regardless of officialdom. Similarly, some took things upon themselves second time around. Before 1939, a TA (Territorial Army) battalion parade in Cambridge had in its rear 250 members of the Cambridgeshire Regiment Old Comrades Association. By 1939 some of these 'old and bold' formed what they called the Wisbech Training Corps. They had leaders and instructors ready-made when Eden broadcast.

A nineteenth-century force, the rifle volunteers, formed in case of a French invasion, were within living memory – just. Surely the oldest defence volunteer of 1940, and an extraordinary link with the mid-Victorian rifle volunteers, was John Davis, who must have called on the Cheltenham daily newspaper's offices even before Eden launched the LDV. The paper's gossip columnist duly reported that the 91-year-old, 'fit and as hearty as can be', was anxious to serve. He had joined the Post Office Rifles in 1868 and claimed to have delivered letters to Charles Dickens.

The authorities already had a defence body without having to set up another: the National Defence Companies. Maxse in his memo recalled a 'rather shadowy force', the Royal Defence Corps, probably 'sadly wasted away' during 'the lean years' between the wars when the government spent so little on the armed forces. In July 1936, as Nazi Germany became to menace, the government announced National Defence Companies of the TA by county or city. Membership by November 1937 was a spectacularly undaunting 6,766. In March 1939, members were asked to do six drills a year – again, hardly anything. Eden and his War Office advisers decided to start from scratch with a new organisation, rather than use the National Defence Companies that no-one had heard of, or the long-forgotten and patchy First World War volunteers.

A DOG'S DINNER; AND HORSEMEN

General Sir Henry Pownall, the chief of staff of the BEF, was put in charge of inspecting the Local Defence Volunteers in June, after the BEF was thrown out of France and evacuated from Dunkirk. In the first entry of his new diary he wrote with characteristic hauteur that Eden had announced the LDV

> … without I gather enough time for previous thought or organisation by the War Office or GHQ Home Forces … The organisation in fact started from below rather than above. The result of course is that it is a rare 'dog's dinner' now.

It was always going to be a dog's dinner, because of the haste, and because so many people were coming together who had never had dealings with each other. According to the notes from a Home Forces conference on 17 May, among other things it urged commanders to 'liaise with everybody, British Legion, National Union of Cyclists have offered their services; make use of every organised body. Must avoid getting duds in.'

Who would call whom a dud? Even cyclists had rival organisations, each ringing their own bells. Herbert Stanier, secretary of the Cyclists Touring Club (CTC); and Adrian Chamberlain, secretary of the National Cyclists Union (NCU) went out of their way in those weeks to write to newspapers around the

Above, left: Webber's Post on Exmoor, no matter how remote the road, signposts came down in case they aided the enemy.

Above, right: An Elan Valley dam in Wales. A target? Germans were not likely to land on the top of a hill in Wales, so General Ironside told Home Guard commanders in June 1940. But local commanders even in the most remote parts of the country sought to patrol the land, sometimes on horse or pony.

country, each boasting about what their organisation was doing for defence (and ignoring their rival). In the weekly *Coalville Times* of 7 June, Chamberlain told how three weeks before, NCU members began patrolling highways for parachutists. Cyclists' mobility was, Chamberlain reckoned, 'of inestimable use to the new local defence volunteer force'. A fortnight later, in the same newspaper, Stanier described CTC members as air raid precaution (ARP) messengers and useful to the 'parashots' – an early name for the anti-parachutist defence volunteers.

Horsemen too claimed a role. On 16 May, Major F.S. James, Sheffield Chief Constable, told the *Yorkshire Post* that as most of the patrolling in the Sheffield area would be on the moors outside the town, a 'mounted detachment' would be invaluable. Sure enough, the *Sheffield Telegraph* printed a photograph of an ex-cavalry man leading a string of riders past his home at Callow. The horsemen had volunteered to cover the moors between Hathersage and Buxton, to watch for paratroopers. To point out only two other mounted patrols, one went around the sparsely populated fringes of Oxford – between villages like Woodeaton, Horton cum Studley, Waterstock and Stadhampton; and another crossed the wildest part of mid-Wales, between Tregaron and River Towy. Horses were the only way to cover such a remote area that was, as a history of Home Guards in Cardiganshire described it, a 'no man's land'.

As with so much about home defence in 1940, many people were having the same idea at once. In June, a Captain Anthony Hope, looking for work, wrote a complaint to the authorities that he was 'not very kindly treated', though he had been twelve years in the Army, three in charge of irregular levies with 'political and intelligence work'. He had an idea for mounted patrols, having had experience on the Persian border with 500 levies. He suggested that horse patrols would conserve machines and watch large areas of the country with economy. 'Local defence people had told me that there is considerable discrepancy between the arrangements of even adjacent villages and that uniformity of procedure and action is not much in evidence.' This prompted Churchill's chief of staff General Ismay to write to General Anderson at the War Office about mounted patrols from riding schools, 'as any suggestion these days is worth considering'.

Separately, a meeting at the War Office on 23 May, mainly of colonels from regional commands, agreed to use the motoring organisations RAC and AA, and pony clubs, as dispatch riders where possible.

POLICE AND PUBS

Arguably the most obvious force to take charge against invasion was the police. They were a uniformed force, already there, official and national, already with assigned tasks in the case of an invasion. In any emergency, the state expected the police to do the dirty jobs.

Len Francis was a Cheltenham Grammar School boy whose father was the police sergeant in the Cotswold village of Winchcombe. Their family home was the living quarters of the police station. By the summer of 1940 the police had issued Len Francis' father with a .45 revolver and he and the other policemen fired it at a target in the orchard behind the police station. Len Francis recalled:

> Being conversant with guns – I had an air-gun and had been out shooting rabbits with a 12 bore shot gun – I was allowed a few shots and was impressed with the recoil the gun gave. I never knew whether my father's revolver was meant to repel German invaders or to quell civic unrest.

That said, police – as their officers made clear – were not part of the armed forces of the Crown. If police were armed, to keep order, that still did not make them part of the armed forces, or able to fight an invader.

One commentator, the broadcaster A.G. Street, paid tribute to the police later in the war, claiming 'in every rural district they were the Home Guard's father, mother and daughter.' Yet, as so often, some would tell another story. Lieutenant-Colonel H.K. Boyle, who raised a company at Moortown in Leeds, recalled he had a mere eighteen rifles at first for perhaps 400 men, covering a two-mile front. Given such a 'desperate and deadly shortage' of guns, his men added 'shotguns, sporting rifles, revolvers and any other weapons that volunteers either possessed or could borrow'. However: 'The police put up a strenuous opposition from the first against these revolvers and the anomalous position was reached of men going out night after night to defend their country against possible enemy paratroops and having to conceal their arms for so doing from our own police.' To Boyle, this was one of the 'stupidities of 1940'. Boyle plainly wanted police to relax the rules on holding guns during the national emergency. Several cases came to court around the country of men carrying a gun or an airgun in public, without a licence. Sometimes the magistrates let the men off, sometimes not.

The police could argue that they were not there to choose which laws to enforce, and nobody told them anything different – or even told them anything – although Eden in his broadcast had asked volunteers to report to their local police station. Just after Eden's broadcast, the Chief Constable of Newark, G.F. Goodman, admitted at Newark town hall to a crowded meeting of ex-servicemen that he did not know much, only that he had been asked to arrange somewhere for volunteers to register. Police were the gate-keepers and simply taking the names and addresses of volunteers would take some doing. Organisers would then look out for likely helpers – and be vigilant in keeping out communists and fascists.

As soon as they came together, volunteers talked. A journalist, John Langdon-Davies, was one of several self-appointed instant authorities on how to counter an invasion. He began one of his 1940 books, *Parachutes over Britain*: 'In the pub tonight most of us are meeting to discuss the formation of a local defence corps of parashots.' As he admitted, this was a chance for men to indulge their imaginations: '… those of us who when younger were Boy Scouts or imagined ourselves to be Red Indians have now got the opportunity to play our boyhood games on a grander scale.'

Pubs were of course the convenient meeting places. Hugh Meynell recalled the Shropshire small town where his father volunteered:

> I would be about ten years old. Albrighton, they used to parade in the car park of the Crown Hotel, every Thursday [evening]. And that was because the men were farm hands or firemen or old fogeys who were too old for the war, so evenings the farm hands were tired out after a day's work or fed up with the thought of going to the Home Guard. I suppose on looking back, all the officers were my father's generation, who had all been serving officers in the First World War. And the company sergeant major was Regimental Sergeant Major Moore, an ex-RSM from the Indian Army. He was a dapper little man, he kept the Crown Hotel in the day time and used to appear wearing a bow tie and a tuxedo and open the doors at 11am and take a huge breath of fresh air and say, that was his fresh air for the day.

The volunteers were good for the pub trade, and made quick and cheap recruits for the state. Were volunteers, though, the right people to counter an invasion? The military theorist Basil Liddell Hart doubted it, with a frankness that he did not – or dared not – show in public. In private notes in June 1940 he wrote of the 'fundamentals of war'.

Men's resistance is strongest when their instincts to defend their country and protect their families coincide and weakest when any conflict is created between these two instincts. When it comes to the point, men who belong to a village may be wary of putting up a resistance within it when that is likely to involve the destruction of their homes and families. Such a difficulty does not arise of course with troops who are merely stationed in the area or brought there in an emergency.

Volunteers would hardly take kindly to going across country to defend strangers, leaving their families behind, merely so they would fight more fiercely; and it was more practical to leave the volunteers where they were, to defend their homes. How much could you reasonably ask of unpaid volunteers, in any case?

1939: THE THREAT DISMISSED

Could the authorities have seen all this coming? Some people reckoned so. Captain D. Bourne, Midland area secretary for the British Legion, was saying in the first days of the LDV, 'when the war started we wanted to do something of this sort.' He was one of those who believed that the British Legion, as veterans of 1914–18, 'should have run the whole show'. Similarly, Stephen Morton, secretary of Sheffield and district federation of the Ramblers Association, claimed he had suggested a 'scheme of service', in other words a watch over the countryside, before the war, but whoever he told in authority had told him to join the forces. Of course such people might have been being wise after the event.

In truth, the military did weigh the risks before the war. According to the official historian of the defence of the UK, successive governments put off attending to coastal defence 'like a man who dreads a visit to the dentist'.

In February 1939, after the War Office asked for a defence review – the question having been discussed in September 1938 – Major-General Green, a Devonport-based commander, replied to a Southern Command letter asking whether garrisons should be mobile. Green wrote: 'I understand that enemy landings have now been practically ruled out of consideration as being unfeasible.' A garrison's main duty, he added, would be to assist civil authorities in the event of air raids. Lieutenant-General A. P. Wavell, then in charge at Southern Command in Salisbury, agreed: 'Personally I feel that the probability of such [hostile] landings is very remote.' A sub-committee of the Committee of Imperial Defence (no less) had ruled that the likelihood of organised attack on a large scale on the shores of Britain was very small, so a Lieutenant-Colonel A. W. Lee of Southern Command's general staff wrote to area commands in March 1939. 'There is however the possibility of small raids carried out by limited numbers of troops transported in fast warships, submarines or possibly dropped by parachutes but it is considered that this is only likely to take place on the east coast.' The east coast, until May 1940, was England's only coast facing the enemy.

Desk wallahs were batting the unlikely risk around on paper, rather than doing very much about it. Air Commodore John Slessor at the Air Ministry raised the possibility of paratroopers in a letter to Brigadier John Kennedy at the War Office on 25 September 1939.

> You will remember I have raised this question of parachute attack on various occasions and if I remember rightly your general view has been that it could be dealt with, if it were successful in dropping a large number of troops, under local district or area defence schemes by the movement to the threatened point of a reserve which is available for the purpose.

Slessor questioned whether any reserve at 'fire brigade readiness' would have transport and communications sufficient to meet possibly 2,000–3,000 invaders. Slessor was arguing it was unwise to ignore the possibility, but it was the Army, not his Air Force, that would have to spare men to watch for parachutes. Instead, even after Germany invaded Norway in April 1940, the military was looking to take soldiers away from home defence, to send fighting men to the Continent. A meeting on 24 April at Horse Guards between General Sir Walter Kirke and his regional commanders heard that the total of 30,500 guards on VPs (vital or vulnerable points), was 6,500 lower than in March 1940. And the Army proposed to release another 3,000 men from guard duties by May. Proposed instead were more dock police and physical defences, to save on men.

1939: THE THREAT WITHIN

At the Home Office on 31 October 1939 civil servants and the military discussed co-operation of the civil authorities in the event of an invasion. The view of the meeting was that 'such enemy action represents a very outside chance'. They agreed on the need to keep roads clear, allay panic and stop evacuation – 'Broadcasts might help here' – and went on: 'What we feel is that the best way in which the civil population can help us to mop up the invaders, which we hope will be only a matter of a few days, is to take refuge in their homes or other shelters and sit quiet until the danger is past.'

Such a condescending official opinion – of civilians at best not getting in the way of those doing the fighting – lingered through 1940, though it did not sit easily with Eden's broadcast appeal.

The authorities, showing even less trust in their own citizens, feared trouble. The military ran a two-day defence exercise in London in April 1939. Officers visited the places they then acted out 'narratives' about. First, the battalion at

Chelsea Barracks had orders to move by river transport to West India Docks, because crowds were trying to get into them. The Army orders were to prevent refugees moving into the Isle of Dogs.

Next, after a heavy air raid, Bond Street and Park Lane had damage, and 'there has been considerable infiltration of doubtful elements from the East End escaping heavily bombed areas and making use of air raid shelters in the West End parks.' Police were afraid of looting of 'jewellers and other high class shops'. The Army's task was to cordon the area. Another narrative: the railway stationmaster at Marylebone rang police, who rang Chelsea Barracks to say that crowds were rushing the station, which was already full of refugees. Because of bomb damage to the line, trains could only use one platform for evacuation. Refugees were breaking windows of the booking hall office to try to get to trains. The Army's job was to clear the station and maintain order, maybe even making a bayonet charge on the crowd.

The Army plainly did not see it as unthinkable that in a second world war they might have to kill their own people. The paperwork went to other Army units, for them to carry out their own exercises. Officers from Wiltshire ran a similar exercise with police in Bristol in June 1939.

These narratives – and by the end of the war there were plenty going over what towns, cities and areas of the countryside would do if the enemy landed, from south Wales to Durham – give an eerie insight into what the writers thought might happen and what commanders ought to think about, just in case. Crowds of evacuees at a railway station might be trampled to death or pushed onto live rails. Crowds in a bombed street might block ambulances and fire engines. Hungry people might loot shops, or rush soup kitchens and warehouses.

That a few months before war broke out Army officers were debating secretly when it was proper to shoot food rioters, says it all about how unprepared Britain was for the conflict. It is difficult after the event to appreciate how extraordinary the German use in May 1940 of paratroopers and troops landing by glider and aeroplane seemed. The *Belfast Telegraph* on 13 May called it 'sinister', as if the Germans were somehow breaking rules so painfully learned in 1914–18.

For some people, the only way to respond was to embrace change, both military and political. Tom Wintringham, another of the year's instant experts, writing in July in a book entitled *New Ways of War*, called for a 'citizens' army' of four million. Wintringham demanded that Britain abandon what he called 'Whitehall methods'. He wanted an end to men and women feeling thwarted and resentful that they were not wanted or consulted. For all some people knew in 1940, this was trouble-making talk that might lead to riots.

Other men grasped that warfare had suddenly been transformed. The Germans were having such success because they fought more three-dimensionally, faster, with insolence, even. Commanders sought to drum the lessons into Britain, as soon as the last boatloads of troops had fled home from Dunkirk. General Ironside,

Above: General Sir William Edmund Ironside at his desk in 1939, as Chief of the Imperial General Staff.

Left: The corner of the Square and Ford Street in Moretonhampstead in Devon, showing a petrol station and stores. As most villages had petrol pumps, the fear was that invaders might steal vehicles and fuel to facilitate their advance.

the new Commander in Chief Home Forces, spoke to local defence volunteer leaders at Chester on 5 June. Only store petrol where you can defend it, he advised, 'because you saw cases in France of the German columns coming up to the wayside pump and the man at the wayside pump with a revolver at his head pumping petrol into the empty tanks. That we must not have.' Wintringham in his book was barking up the same tree: 'Britain and the people who live in Britain can be made safe. But the changes necessary to give us that safety are enormous.'

The Germans caught Britain unprepared, then, on 10 May 1940. That was nothing new for Britain – when was it ever ready for a war? Some even took comfort from that, believing that England would win in the end.

The unsettling difference was that the country had to work fast this time, against a threat that could snuff the life out of the country in the hour or two it would take troop-carrying aircraft to cross the Channel. The shock of paratroopers soon faded – only because worse danger followed.

CHAPTER 2

THE NEXT SHOCK: BRITAIN ALONE

It's very difficult for old people, for old men particularly, in a war. They cannot grow accustomed to the fact that there is little they can do to help; they suffer from frustration; and the war eats into them.

Nevil Shute, *Pied Piper* (1942)

For all Churchill's fame, it was Anthony Eden, the new Secretary of State for War, who went on the radio on 14 May to make what proved to be the all-important appeal for 'local defence volunteers'. While it is possible to find contrary views about almost everything that happened in Britain in 1940, all the newspapers of the day, the histories afterwards and the recollections of men who were there, agree: Eden drew an immediate, large and enthusiastic response. It is pointless to speculate who did so first – certainly some men did not wait for the end of the broadcast to run out of the house to volunteer.

Partly, men felt the basic urge to defend their homes. Some of those volunteering were (like Eden) of the generation that had fought in 1914–18 as young men and were now in middle age, usually too old to join the military again. As the Cambridgeshire Home Guard historian put it: 'Although in the years after 1918 many of them had said never again, they responded almost to a man when once more their country was in danger.'

They longed to do something useful. John Howard, the elderly hero of Shute's novel *Pied Piper*, begins the summer of 1940 listening to all the radio news and in between the bulletins he reads the papers and worries. At least one newspaper sensed this in the real world: 'Who is more "up to German tricks" than the old soldier and who is more ready to counter them? … No German who descends from the skies by parachute will go undetected. The old soldiers, now young again, will see to that.'

Yoxall, Staffordshire Home Guard. 'Pop' Lester – the uniformed man with the walrus moustache kneeling – was 70 in 1940.

Newspapers meanwhile made much of the refugees fleeing from the German advance, who in turn made much of the paratroopers. Even the smallest local newspaper seemed able to find a refugee with a local angle; everyone from salesmen to the Sadlers Wells ballet company on tour and former Arsenal footballer Fred Pagnam, coaching in Holland. The papers printed the dottiest stories as gospel. A Rolls-Royce engineer from Derby, living in Belgium for ten years, Dundonald Jackson, described being machine-gunned by German aeroplanes as he fled. He claimed that a crowd captured a German parachutist who was wearing Belgian native cycling costume. The Belgians, so the story went, recognised the enemy by a large elastic band around his waist. What did readers make of it? That paratroopers wore elastic bands – or that Belgian cyclists did not? The older you were, the more difficult it was to take in at once, and the easier it was to fear that it could happen in Britain.

In 1940 Dr Jack Longley was 66; he had retired to the Bristol suburb of Westbury on Trym. He wrote in his diary for Thursday 16 May:

Terrible battle now in progress in Belgium. The German hoards [sic] have over-run Holland and the Queen and Government have had to escape to England.

Post-war French fishing vessels at Newlyn harbour, Cornwall. The swift German conquest of western Europe brought boatloads of refugees from several countries – which only added to English fears of enemy agents.

If the Allies cannot force them back we shall soon have our own dear land invaded, the first time since 1066 … put in six tomato plants today. The bed of tulips still look lovely. A beautiful day with nature looking at its loveliest. Can it be possible that we shall be treated like Belgium and all God's beautiful objects be defiled by man's abomination. God forbid.

So Dr Longley wrung his hands, bewildered by current affairs, not that it put him off his gardening – and sport. He also wrote that he had a round of golf with Mr Ayres, a retired Baptist minister: 'He beat me badly.'

Partly out of vanity, partly because no-one could know for sure, everybody worried aloud that their part of the country was at risk of invasion, if not first, then eventually. The *Yorkshire Evening Press* gave its opinion on 15 May, the day after Eden's speech: 'A large part of this county is sparsely populated. There are great areas of moorland and fell and wide expanses of cultivated land where disguised troops might be landed from the air.' The *Sussex Express and County Leader* on 17 May told its readers: 'It is in seaboard counties like Sussex with open spaces favouring attempts at parachute landings that the defence force is most needed.'

The gatehouse to the Bishop's Palace and Vicars' Close in Wells. Such was the fear of paratroopers landing in remote countryside that in his 14 May broadcast launching the Local Defence Volunteers, Eden implied that only sleepy country places like Wells needed volunteers, not England's main cities.

In between, the Lord Lieutenant of Lincolnshire, Lord Brownlow, wrote of the danger to his county, the second largest in England, 'and as far as this new threat is concerned … definitely "in the firing line" for we have a coastline well over 100 miles and the more remote the villages or districts the greater the likelihood of an attempt [by parachutists].'

At least one Home Guard historian (in Abingdon) admitted the funny side of it afterwards: 'We all knew anyhow that priorities or no priorities ours was the one spot in the whole kingdom that quite certainly was clearly marked on the operational maps of the German high command.'

Newspapers both fed the speculation and fed off it and privately some really quite senior people, though military amateurs, felt they ought to pass on their theories to government. Labour MP Ellen Wilkinson, on 28 May 1940, sent to Churchill a typed paper given to her by 'a Scottish doctor with German connections and who has made a study of strategy as a hobby … There may be nothing in it but I felt you ought to see it,' she wrote. The paper warned of capture of the 'narrow waist' of Scotland by paratroopers, or seaplanes on the firths. You only have to glance at a map to see that was hardly the most obvious threat to the British Isles. Lieutenant-Colonel Ian Jacob passed it to a Major Hutchinson at the War Office. Hutchinson answered with a sigh: 'Just another of the many brainwaves which are fired at us from time to time – I wonder if Miss Ellen Wilkinson has any particular interest thereabouts as it may only be a ways and means of getting more troops stationed in the locality.'

To be fair, the generals and politicians too were hedging their bets about where invasion might come. An early Royal Navy study of a possible invasion, coincidentally also dated 28 May 1940, began: 'To achieve the greatest measure of surprise, it is likely that the enemy will use the shortest sea route to his objective.' It added that the 'possibility of diversions or subsidiary operations in the Shetlands, Ireland, or north of Scotland, must be borne in mind'. The most favourable area for the invader apparently ran from the Wash to Newhaven 'and will grow to the west according to the enemy progress in France'. Pownall wrote in his diary in June:

> … as to landing troops he [Hitler] knows we expect him on the east and south east coasts and probably exaggerates the strength with which we could meet him. He may go therefore for the south and south west but if he does I should not be in the least surprised if he went also for Ireland. There he can walk in for the asking. There are plenty of fifth column there already I have no doubt apart from the IRA, a very happy hunting ground for him. If he gets hold of Ireland he would be round us on three sides.

All the uncertainty filtered down to the man in the street. George Lane, a 32-year-old watch and clock repairer in Kidderminster, wrote in his diary on

26 June 1940 – the day after he had reported for LDV duty – 'it is thought that the enemy will try to occupy Ireland as the next step, probably helped of course from within.'

ISLES OF SCILLY – ANOTHER WALK-OVER?

While people great and small speculated, Germany conquered France by mid-June. By the end of the month the enemy took command of the coastline facing Britain. The Channel Islands, so close to France, were beyond defending. At the end of June, the Germans sailed in. Could the same have happened to the Isles of Scilly?

The Army's Southern Command wrote to the Admiral commanding Western Approaches (in charge of the sea around the Scillies) as early as 29 May, asking if the isles should be defended. To do so adequately would require at least a battalion, the Army said, and no troops were available. It sounded like the Army was doing some lobbying, and it worked. By 7 June the RAF and Royal Navy had undertaken the defence of the Scillies. Little if anything came of that, though. By 9 July the Army was reporting that the LDV on the isles had 157 enrolled men. More or less all of them had uniforms – 150 denim suits – but they were hardly bristling with arms. They had eight rifles, plus another 20 from Southern Command, and 37 shotguns of their own. Southern Command added, in case anyone thought the Army should have done more: 'Considering how few there are of them their treatment has been most generous in arms and equipment compared with other zones.' In notes dated 16 July the Army gave two reasons to defend the Isles of Scilly: the Germans would gain a useful submarine base; and further surrender of British territory (after the Channel Islands fell without a shot) would have a bad effect on morale. There was a population of 1,750, a dozen beaches 'landable', and an aerodrome, obstructed at night. And as Southern Command wrote on 15 July, morale was said to be good but the residents felt 'some apprehension' that they might suffer the same fate as the Channel Islands. As the Army felt it necessary to give reasons why the isles should be defended, this begs the question whether those in charge were actually willing to do it.

The Army sent a company of 180 commandos to the Isles of Scilly on 19 July. A lieutenant-colonel reported on 17 July how a Major Arthur Dorrien-Smith, of Tresco Abbey, organiser of the now 173 LDVs, had worked out defence down to the last detail. 'He is however of a certain age,' the officer reported diplomatically, implying Dorrien-Smith was far too old. His second in command, a Reverend D. Paghe, was 'an ex-Warrant Officer … but over 70'. About 40 per cent of the LDV were ex-soldiers; 'all questioned seem very keen.' They were manning four posts dusk to dawn. Every LDV was in possession of a 'weapon of sorts'. If the Germans landed, the Army promised to relieve the defenders in 24 hours, from the mainland. That was an empty, even cynical promise, because Lieutenant-General

Two views of the Lizard lighthouse at the tip of Cornwall. Defences here and on the Isles of Scilly were thin all summer because there were not enough troops to go round.

Franklyn of 8 Corps (covering that region) wrote to his superiors at Southern Command on 2 September that if the enemy succeeded in landing, fighting on the isles would be all over in a few hours. It would then take a brigade to recapture St Mary's, the main island. The day after, Franklyn told Southern Command that he only had six battalions in reserve and to send one to the isles was dangerous. Already he had a pioneer battalion on the coast between Sidmouth and Seaton and in his view such recruits ought not to hold that important sector, at the hinge of the 'Taunton stop line'. Franklyn, in other words, was making the best case he could for some extra soldiers.

Meanwhile in London, the War Cabinet agreed on 30 August – months after a few hundred Germans could have walked in – that the Isles of Scilly should be held at all costs.

FORECASTING

Some sought to play down the risk. 'It would be exceedingly difficult for an enemy to attack the Isle of Wight in any strength,' the *County Press* told its readers on 1 June, when surely the opposite was true. The enemy could easily land on the beaches or piers around the island, or drop as many men as it liked by parachute on the sparsely-populated downs in the middle. That was the problem; for all anybody knew, an invader could land on any beach, or parachute into any field, even if they if they simply sailed or blew off course. Hence a dozen trains, grouped in fours, patrolled the south and east coast between Plymouth and Perth. Mainly manned by Polish troops, all the trains were kept constantly under steam until June 1941.

Handicapping the Army, Navy and Royal Air Force alike was the difficulty of forecasting where Hitler would strike first, or hardest. Men and machines were so short that there was no way to cover every possibility. In June 1940, the Admiralty was arguing about where to place warships. Should the battleships *Nelson*, *Rodney*

Above: 9.2-inch gun crew taking post at Culver Point Battery, eastern Isle of Wight. (War Office official photograph, 24 August 1940)

Left: The sands at Paignton. In their planning the Germans – like the Allies when invading France in 1944 – chose wide beaches for easier landing of troops and tanks, backed by paratroop drops inland. Both sides used picture postcards to help their invasion planning.

and *Ark Royal* stay at Scapa, and the fastest battle cruisers at Rosyth, in Scotland, so that they would sail south in time to intercept the German navy aiding a south or east coast invasion? There were no capital (that is, heaviest) ships in Dover force, and the Navy would rely on the Dover barrage, aircraft, motor torpedo boats and destroyers to prevent a German naval breakout down the Channel. The Admiralty admitted the defences of Plymouth were 'inadequate', but the Navy might have to risk stationing heavy ships there. South-west Ireland was an obvious place as a capital ship base but the Irish were suffering from 'incredible short-sightedness' – in other words, they would not give their ports to the English. On 1 June 1940 the Commander in Chief Home Fleet told the Admiralty that he could not give final information about what ships would go where until he knew what other forces – RAF and Army – were available for UK defences.

Nobody wanted to be the one who made a wrong decision, let the invaders in, and lost Britain the war. But defenders had to go somewhere. John Langdon-Davies was alive to this dilemma in his 1940 book *Parachutes over Britain*: 'Of course nothing serious will happen to more than a few dozen of Britain's thousands of towns and villages. The trouble is that nobody can say beforehand which few dozen will be singled out.'

It was easy for some people to find shortcomings and complain about them, difficult to dismiss or ignore because the carping was in the name of helping win the war. On 22 July 1940 a letter went to Nottingham's clerk, Mr J.E. Richards, from M.F.M. (Montague) Wright, of Butterley Colliery, and Chief Special Constable for the Ollerton district, about events the previous evening. Mr Wright had arrived with a police sergeant at Boughton waterworks belonging to Nottingham council at 9.45pm. The gate was open, and the two men walked to the main pump house. There, four men, obviously workers changing shifts, were sitting in a corner, talking. Mr Wright fumed: 'I spoke to these men about the position in which they had put themselves as if I had had a gun I could have been in full command of the pumping station having got into the main pump house without seeing anyone or being challenged.' Having given the workers a lesson in Nazi waterworks-capturing tactics, the two left. One of the workers said they had orders to lock at 10pm; so they did. 'I do not like bringing complaints of this sort to your notice,' Mr Wright said, although he came across as the sort of busybody who, in fact, did like it, 'but I do think something ought to be done to strengthen the look-out of this very vulnerable point.'

Rather than quibble about whether a Midlands waterworks was worth bothering about, Mr Richards passed Mr Wright's letter to Nottingham City Council water engineer B.W. Davies, who wrote to Richards on 25 July, agreeing that the waterworks was vulnerable. Guards, he reported, had to be provided by station staff, and adequate patrolling was impossible. 'Had the LDV recruited from Mr Wright's colliers not been withdrawn from assisting in the protection of the works, the state of affairs reported by Mr Wright should not have been possible,' Mr Davies wrote, tartly.

THE POLITICIAN PROBLEM

Some senior politicians gave in to the same urge to point things out, somewhat apologetically, from which we can infer that they were only telling the generals things they already knew. On India Office notepaper minister Leo Amery wrote to General 'Pug' Ismay on 27 May:

A friend of mine was on Romney Marsh yesterday and very much impressed by the wonderful landing ground it would make for parachutists and by the relative absence of any forces of ours on the spot. Parachutists landing there and seizing Ashford Junction might be an awkward thing. Anyhow I pass it on for what it is worth. No reply.

At the Cabinet Office, Jacob noted drily in ink: 'I suggest you take him at his word.' The by then Lord Ismay did not include this in his 1960 memoirs.

Others, too, got unsolicited mail from bright sparks. On 31 May G.E. Jukes of York suggested an extra use for the BBC to General Jack Dill, Chief of the Imperial General Staff, and Sir John Anderson, the Home Secretary. Instead of the BBC closing between 12.15am and 7am, the radio should have an announcer giving the time signal every 15 minutes. If the government knew the enemy was arriving, it could give notice. The LDV could arrange for women volunteers to listen in, near a motorcyclist or car who would tell LDV of the neighbourhood and the village postmistress. What if the enemy was to arrive between 7am and midnight? Mr Jukes had thought of that too. Stop the programme at the next quarter hour and give the order, he said. Nothing came of it.

MPs were a threat to government getting on with whatever it wanted to do, even if it was only by stopping ministers or their officials in the corridors of Whitehall and moaning at them, as one did in March 1942 to Home Secretary Herbert Morrison's private secretary. The MP complained that regional commissioners setting up 'invasion committees' in some areas were not keeping MPs sufficiently informed. Each regional commissioner had important tasks if an invasion (or indeed later on, a nuclear war) meant that central government could no longer function. This prompted the Ministry of Home Security to ask each regional commissioner's office how many MPs had taken up earlier invitations to be briefed about invasion. It turned out that MPs had never taken much interest. Some regions' replies went as far back as 1940. Nottingham region for example had invited its 39 MPs to three meetings; at the first, in August 1940, only eleven attended. Similarly, in Leeds, only a minority of MPs ever accepted invites to meet, even in June and July 1940, when 15 and 25 accepted, out of 52 Yorkshire MPs. To be fair, some were ministers busy in London, or on active service. Some MPs, though – and some regional offices had taken the precaution of keeping a note – just did not bother.

Another way of shutting politicians up was to give them a job. Pownall in his first diary entry of 20 June as inspector-general of the Local Defence Volunteers (soon renamed Home Guards) went over the first five weeks of the LDV. He wrote that there was hope of co-opting MPs with military experience: 'They may as well do something useful instead of meeting by the hundred to grouse!' This was, Pownall added, an idea warmly welcomed by Edward Grigg, Eden's Under Secretary of State for War, 'if only because it gives employment (unpaid!) to two ex-Cabinet ministers'.

BIRTH PANGS

Pownall had dropped into the top of an organisation that had already gone through weeks of birth pangs. A lord lieutenant officially had the task of setting up the defence volunteers in each county. Usually they passed the job on – to other local aristocrats, land-owners, and people of power and influence, who often had high military rank from 1914–18 (or earlier). A War Office telegram of 18 May set out that the LDV was part of the armed forces and subject to military law. But control, so central government said, should be simple, decentralised, 'with the minimum of regulations and formalities'. A section – the most basic unit of defence volunteers, as in the Army – should be of about ten men, grouped in platoons, and into companies. As for paperwork, the government was only proposing an 'enrolment form'. Helpfully, the War Office sent a specimen.

Men often came together earliest in the county towns. Trowbridge, in Wiltshire, had manned observation posts on higher ground outside the town at Trowle, West Ashton and Steeple Ashton, from 21/22 May. Each post had six rifles, ten rounds of ammunition each and for uniform, seven caps and seven armbands. That is, enough for seven men on guard at any time. The men also carried home-made coshes.

How fast men came together and did something, depended on each organiser. As for what the men ought to do, as an LDV conference heard on 23 May at the War Office, it was 'self-evident that functions of LDV had not received proper consideration'. The day began with progress reports 'required by politicians' (so the military grumbled), for example on numbers of people enrolled and numbers of firearms issued. Names, so notes of the meeting suggested, were 'academic' but recorded to satisfy a 'craving in certain places for tidy organisation'.

Everything was starting from scratch. The organisation was so novel it did not even have its own notepaper. Sir Hereward Wake, writing to Southern Command on 29 May, used Northamptonshire Territorial Army Association headed notepaper with the last three words crossed out, and 'LDV' written in ink above. Pownall grumbled in his diary on 20 June about the 'tremendous amount of work to be done getting the show pulled together and sorted out'. A supposedly national organisation with so little to go on was bound to have what Pownall called 'local complications'. He complained that 'the lords lieutenant have already had an oar in it particularly in the matter of patronage; a rather dangerous affair.' A fortnight later, the first 'major trouble' he listed was 'the indifferent personnel who got office by patronage and otherwise in the first instance … they now constitute a vested interest. Many of them are local worthies or retired generals or may be important employers of labour. It is a difficult problem to shift them …'

Who were these 'indifferent personnel'? While it is unfair to single out anyone, conider Colonel F.B. Leyland of Weston Hall, Bulkington in Nuneaton. A newspaper in the town spoke of his qualities as a local leader. 'As a rider to hounds

Three views of Truro: the cathedral from Kenwyn Hill; Malpas Road outside the city; and Malpas. Unfortunately, the empty spaces that Eden wanted volunteers to guard were miles away from the people volunteering to do the guarding.

he has also gained a unique knowledge of the countryside around Nuneaton which should stand him in good stead if he is called upon to hunt down enemy parachute troops'. It escaped the newspaper that a poacher might have as good knowledge of the country, though not the social standing. Besides, unlike a fox, German paratroopers would presumably fight back.

Organisers, in a word, were looking for people like themselves. There was an appeal, for example, in Carlisle's evening newspaper for a commander for the Silloth Company LDV. It is striking how vague the appeal was. Names had to go to Major Ronald Carr, at Carr's biscuit factory in Carlisle. Silloth, on the north Cumbrian coast is isolated, and we can only assume organisers in the nearest city of Carlisle had no-one in mind. The only requirement was that you had to be an ex-officer or senior non-commissioned officer.

SELF-HELP

The first reaction of some was not even to band together, but for each man to fight his own corner. W. A. J. Archbold of Cambridge had a letter printed in *The Times* of 15 May, probably written just before Eden's broadcast: 'We are constantly told that the Germans are going to drop men into our back gardens,' he claimed. He suggested that people like himself who had shot, 'indifferently it is true, in many parts of the world, should be given rifles and ammunition. As things are, I should have to go at him [a parachutist] with a rolling pin.'

The authorities would not stand for such anarchy. If people wanted to resist, with guns, they had to join a state-run body, and carry only the state's firearms – although in the first chaotic months, the state turned a blind eye to home-made bombs, booby-traps, or 'cocktails'.

Factory units were best placed to make their own weapons. Fred Barratt and workmates made up an LDV unit at their Wednesfield, West Midlands engineering works:

> We never had to turn out, but if we did, it was who learned the fastest; it was improvisation, a hell of a lot. The works units had quite a lot of opportunities for doing all sorts of things, very unorthodox some of it; whether it would have worked? It might have done.

His unit experimented with explosives in fields, having made bombs of acetylene gas, because the works used acetylene for welding.

'A lad in the tool-room said his father had some rifles' – short barrelled, deactivated Martini Henry cavalry carbines – 'which are ideal for the lads of the Boys Brigade, to do arms drill.' The men repaired them at the works and made slings, to use them for drill, and scrounged .303 ammunition from another engineering factory working on a light machine-gun.

Fred Barratt and his fellows made also 'quite a few Bowie knives, made out of old files'. Fred Barratt 'made one or two bottles up of petrol and a bit of stuff'.

> I know one idea I had, half a dozen bottles, didn't need much water; I experimented up the field. Got a box with just small pieces of carbide of calcium because we had barrels of the stuff. And just drop down the neck of a bottle. It had to be dropped down quick with a screw-top bottle; and sling it. They were a first class bomb, you know, because when we were at school we used to do that with small medicine bottles and drop them in the pond. It fetched the fish up!

The same self-help applied to road blocks. However, quite soon the authorities frowned on any improvisation if it threatened the longstanding state monopoly on armies. A typed unsigned letter dated 22 June 1940 by the LDV Leicester city group complained of difficulty because factories 'not vitally important' were organising their own staff as static guards and asking for city volunteers to be released to them. Some were expecting arms. The letter added: 'It has been impressed on us that private armies cannot be allowed.'

That said, a wise Home Guard unit historian recalled that in the early days, real authority was in the hands of those who had intelligence and initiative to act, even if they did not have official authority; because of the urgency felt at the time, many co-operated.

Theft was one way of gaining the initiative. A.J. Yeatman was a LDV then a Home Guard in north Bristol. His platoon 'contained a wonderful selection of characters' including a businessman. 'Volunteer Scantlebury was a cheerful old boy who could wangle all sorts of useful building materials for our HQ etc.' A platoon commander in part of Edgware on the self-mockingly titled 'North West (London) Frontier' was S.B. Hereford, who admitted in his unit's history that in his first speech to his men he warned that time was short and they might be irritated by 'inefficiency of those above us'. His unit built three strong-points with 'ample material' such as railway sleepers, collected 'when no-one was looking'.

Who could join in? Any adult Englishman, so Eden said on the radio –ruling out women. Organisations tried to steal each other's men. So wrote Colonel W.E. Hume-Spry, the head of civil defence for Battle Rural District Council in Sussex, in August 1940. In June, he had not objected to ARP men volunteering for the LDV, because he had thought Home Guard service was part-time. Experience had shown it was not possible to serve in both. He complained

> I am informed that some members of the Home Guard, and Battle parish LDV organiser J.P. Woodhams in particular, are endeavouring to persuade members of the ARP service to resign from the ARP on the grounds that the ARP service can be manned by old men and by women and that wardens are not serving the best interests of their country by remaining with the ARP and that in the event of invasion the ARP service will be taken over by the military etc etc.

Police tried to poach too. According to his memoirs typed at the end of the war, Stroud man E.J. White didn't hear Eden on the radio. He might have become a special constable, because a local detective (and friend) asked what he was doing for the war effort and White promised to join the police specials. Meanwhile White got a postcard asking him to report to Stroud police station, to help with LDV enrolments. As a sergeant during the First World War, he became at once one of the town's six section leaders.

You could forgive such a free-for-all because of the sheer confusion. At the time, who was to say that the LDV would become the Home Guard, a million-man organisation? Tellingly, newspapers at first were so unsure about the LDV that they did not even agree on a name, even in the same paper. You might read of a 'volunteer defence force' on one page, and a volunteer defence corps and a local defence corps on another.

UNIFORMS

It did cross volunteers' minds that to be a proper soldier you had to have a proper uniform. One of the many self-help books rushed into print in 1940, *The Defence of Bloodford Village*, by Colonel G.A. Wade, ran neatly through the many worries of a typical village commander, by the name of 'Skipper Gee' in the fictional 'Bloodford'. Gee, after eating cheese late one night, had one dream after another – an imaginative way to teach bloody truths about counter-invasion. Gradually, Gee learned from each dream to iron out the village defenders' shortcomings. In his second dream, the Germans made Gee a prisoner without his uniform. He said he had not had time to put it on, to 'a chorus of German laughter'. The dreaming Gee saw himself put against the wall and 'ruthlessly shot' and his body hoisted high on a gibbet.

Putting on a uniform not only (so you hoped) saved you from a German bullet if you fell into their hands; it changed men from civilians into at least the makings of soldiers. So suggested Fred Barratt, an original member of the LDV in Wednesfield. He recalled he heard Eden on the radio: 'I was on my bike, straight to Wolverhampton police station; quite a crowd there as well.' As a foreman in his mid-twenties at his factory, he became a sergeant in a platoon of about 40 men. At first, he recalled 'We had no uniform; all we had sent down was an armband, LDV. This is quite true.' Barratt recalled he and other section sergeants told the men: 'you are in uniform now, you are in the Army, and you obey commands.'

It helped that the organisers leaned on First World War veterans, who needed less training in handling a rifle, and in the more subtle acceptance of orders from others in uniform. However sketchy the organisation, tactics and weapons, any unit needed enough uniforms for active men, to identify who was and was not one of them. In Doncaster for example, of 1,200 enrolments at the police station, commanders selected only 240 ex-servicemen for two (north and south) platoons. The first uniforms came by June, and had to pass from sentry to sentry. And yet when in July Doncaster LDV made its first written operational orders, and told its men to wear uniform during civilian hours, it attracted 'undeserved attention and some criticism', according to a later unit history. What did some civilians dislike – the reminder of the war? Did they fear that their workplace might become a battlefield? Or were some guards showing off?

A uniform, more positively, brought pride and togetherness. Men did have to get over their self-consciousness first. Harold Jager, a Cheshire Home Guard historian, recalled that his unit, on first meeting on 23 May, went straight to the local golf course on the Wirral to patrol with white handkerchiefs bound on sleeves. Even

From the June 1941 Rolleston and Stretton Home Guard exercise; a group of First World War veterans.

such a simple sign marked men as a group, men that had to get to know one another. Roll call was a 'most entertaining and humorous ceremony … we gradually learnt to know each other's names … always a painful process for an Englishman.'

Not that the men did anything very military at first, or even for a while. In the village of Aldsworth near Cirencester, Jim Trinder's father was a pigman. On LDV duty he used to go out with a stick tied across the cross-bar of his bicycle. Jim remembered 'a Sunday morning that was the big thing, backwards and forwards, presenting arms and all that. Then they used to dismiss and I expect most of them went to the pub.'

John Hindle, a wartime schoolboy in the village of Poringland near Norwich, recalled something similar. Sometimes the village's Home Guard put a barrier across the street at the church corner, 'the usual farm hurdles and barbed wire':

> There the Home Guard stopped everybody crossing the Church Corner from any direction and demanded to check their ID card (but not us boys). Anybody without their identity card, even people well known to the Home Guard (friends or neighbours) would be held in custody in the guardroom (barn) for a few hours, to make the point that ID cards should be carried at all times. Some Home Guard were right little Hitlers, once they had a uniform and a little authority.

What made farm and factory workers tick as soldiers? A piece of cloth as a uniform, and the comradeship of sticking to the rules, and yet bending them to absurdity, in defiance of (usually invisible) officers. Ron West, a nineteen-year-old carpenter's apprentice in Newport, Isle of Wight, found it so. With a khaki arm-band with the black letters 'LDV', a rifle and five rounds of ammunition as one of the town's first invited volunteers, he came home from work to find an envelope.

You are to report to the Carisbrooke deep water pump house at 10pm for guard duty to 6am. Bring rifle and ammunition, plus haversack rations and sign the chitty to claim ration allowance of one and sixpence for purchase of food. Haversack ration was sandwiches. The problem was what to put in them as food was on ration. All mum had was one egg – so one boiled egg sandwich in two slices of bread. My mother was humorous. It appears you are a secret agent – have you got to eat the note?

On going through the hassle of a young boy carrying a .303 rifle through two road blocks, I soon found out they [Ron's new comrades] were the experts when it came to slipping past Army road blocks – that's another subject.

Stepping through the doorway, an old gentleman sitting behind a table. You are Ron West? Yes. Whilst you are with us you will be called the boy and treated as a boy. Now stand to one side and take note of what I am doing. Now I learnt later in the Army – they produce a drill for every occasion – all to a rhythm of 1-2-3 pause (known as bullshit baffles brains). They were all ex long time serving soldiers who were unofficially back in the ways of the Army. All young in heart – but not in body. Enjoying it. Now it was my turn. I simply place my lunchbox on the table and started to take the sandwiches out to show him. His hand stopped me from lifting them out – paid me my one shilling and sixpence. With a very firm voice: 'As your mother has had to find the money to buy the food you will give it to her. My duty is to sign my life away that you have brought haversack rations. I do not need to know what's in them.' Now dad had warned me that whatever this crowd does, they will make sure the steel plate is in position [that is, in the trousers, covering the bottom]. Even in my innocence there was the smell of a swindle. But the inspection was 100 per cent as laid down by the authorities, no-one could complain. He then got another old boy to explain to me on the subject of haversack rations.

The drill, first man in approached the table, pause 1-2-3. Place lunch box on table pause 1-2-3, remove lid pause 1-2-3-4-5-6, during this long pause the old gentleman would press his finger on the top slice of bread. On went the lid, pause 1-2-3. Hand over the ration chit, pause 1-2-3. Arm bent at the elbow, hand flat and open, ready to receive the one shilling and sixpence.

These First World War veterans knew only that they had to abide by the 'King's rules and regulations'. The old soldiers could turn the rules to advantage. The veteran lifted out of his lunchbox two dry slices of bread, with a layer of newspaper in between. The one and six was beer money. No wonder Ron West's father, a Territorial Army man home on a weekend pass, was surprised that his son had

The stand-down parade of D company, 19 Battalion Royal Hampshire Regiment Home Guard marching with fixed bayonets past the Drill Hall in Newport, Isle of Wight. When Ron West reported for duty as a teenage LDV in the town in 1940, he found old soldiers enjoying themselves hugely by bending the rules.

a rifle without paperwork, or an oath of allegiance to King and Country. 'So father's advice was: see all, hear all, but most of all keep your mouth shut. With this lot you will survive.'

Higher in social standing and more well known, but with the same male drive for clubbing together, was the Upper Thames Patrol (UTP). Sir Ralph Glyn MP set up a patrol of leisure boaters. A rear-admiral was in command and a vice-admiral his assistant. At the end of July the patrol was a guard of honour when King George VI, the Queen, and the Princesses Elizabeth and Margaret went on a pleasure cruise from Windsor. The local paper noted that 'the members of the UTP looked smart in their yachting caps and blue reefer jackets'. If it all sounded like something out of Gilbert and Sullivan – the day before the 'armada of motor-boats' had had a parade ending with tea by ladies of Henley Sailing Club – the volunteers of 1940 (and later) sometimes did have a dressed-up, theatrical air.

LOCAL KNOWLEDGE

What did the LDVs offer, apart from an excuse to earn expenses, or to go boat-ing? The answer is in the name 'LDV'. Lieutenant-General Auchinleck, in a

September order to his Southern Command defined the by then Home Guards as a 'voluntary and localised force' not to be used far from men's homes. The men could 'carry out surprise attacks and ambushes against small parties of enemy', or were 'admirably fitted to act with other troops, as observers, guides, scouts and messengers'.

For example, an LDV man, Jim Honeysett of Wartling, near Herstmonceux in East Sussex, recalled his parish overlooked Pevensey marshes: 'We were used by the regular army to help with their training because the marshes were difficult to cover if you didn't know where you were going.'

But some volunteers needed help even to manage that. A Stroud Home Guard unit historian recalled how in 1940 men got to know their neighbourhood on Sunday mornings. 'It was remarkable how little some knew of their own locality.'

Whatever the locality – a patch of countryside, a part of town, a factory – enough people, somebody, knew the area well enough to make plans to defend it. Reg Titt, a scientist at Porton Down, was a 24-year-old LDV in Salisbury. He recalled:

A few of us had specific duties in the event of invasion. My duty was to render it impossible to get petrol out of the only petrol station in our sector, by unscrewing a pipe junction and ramming lead wool down the pipe. I never saw the lead wool, nor the pipe junction and had no idea what sort of a ramrod would be needed.

Know thine enemy: hence the publication of national official training instructions. Number two, dated June 1940, told its readers – most likely only commanders, such booklets would seldom reach the ranks – that the Germans were in the habit of dropping spies, saboteurs and agents behind the lines 'and may do so in this country. Such men are often dressed in mufti, our own uniform or may assume almost any disguise e.g. priests and even women.' In a way it does not matter whether there was any truth in such stories; what mattered at the time was that the British took them seriously. Already these instructions were discussing the enemy's 'likely forms of attack'.

German plans for the invasion of this country will have been worked out in great detail and secrecy. They will almost certainly combine bombardment from the air with attempted invasion by sea and airborne troops. The main object of the first troops is to prepare the way for further reinforcements. Thus a usual role for parachutists is to capture an aerodrome or improvised landing ground to which more troops may be brought by transport aeroplanes. The whole force might then try to seize a port at which they may hope to get ashore heavy equipment such as guns and tanks with a view to subsequent major operations against our forces.

A scene from the Cannock Home Guard history. A sergeant leads his men into a canal at night. Local knowledge was, however, prized as the one thing the defenders had that the invaders lacked.

German paratroopers on the Continent had prompted the formation of the LDV. Yet within a few weeks, German tanks had cut off the BEF from the main French army, and the BEF left France with what it could carry. That left the UK with what the official historian later termed a 'lamentable shortage' of armour. If a defence lacked mobility, would enemy tanks run riot as they did in France?

'NO MORE ROWS'

The authorities sought both static defence, by the LDV, and a mobile regular army to bring relief. Or so officers heard at a conference with the commander in chief General Ironside at York's Theatre Royal, according to rough notes dated 9 June from LDV Northumbria area headquarters, based at Darlington. The event was secret enough that LDV officers went in 'mufti', in plain clothes. They heard that the LDV was an integral and important part of the British Army. 'Blocks' were the order in rural areas – 'hold him [the enemy] everywhere to give time for our mobile columns to arrive … no private armies or odd mobile columns.' The authorities only wanted military units under their control, though they did embrace one irregular weapon, the 'molotov cocktail' or petrol bomb, that if dropped on a tank immobilised the crew (so the throwers hoped). And the commander in chief did want to rouse all the people to the threat: 'Make the people realise this war is upon us and what has happened on the Continent can happen here. If we do not win, no more liberty!'

Better known than the York meeting is an earlier one, on 5 June, in Chester. Ironside's one hour talk was printed as a booklet, and circulated 'only for LDV'. He said: 'Do not let us have among you people what I shall call council rows.' Don't argue, he appealed, over how to build a trench, or where. At York, he asked his listeners not to fight amongst themselves; 'We are all trying and working at speed to beat the Boche. There may be mistakes but be patient and let no man quarrel with another.' It's always doubtful quite how many people read or heard anything that year, written or spoken by Churchill or anybody else. What evidence there is suggests that Ironside's words went down well. At Doncaster, the town commander read aloud Ironside's speech in the Mansion House, which raised the enthusiasm of the volunteers to 'fever heat', the unit historian later recalled.

Some enthusiasts soon became disillusioned. Eric Pochin, director of a stone breaking machinery manufacturer in Leicester, and a First World War veteran, became second in command of a Leicester LDV platoon. He typed a letter of complaint on 5 July to his company commander, asking for 'instant action … In the first inadequate issue of rifles there was no equipment for cleaning nor were the arms provided with slings.' This was 'slipshod … an intolerable state of affairs', detracted from efficiency, and brought ridicule. Pochin did get a reply, of

Sappers of 211 Field Park Company, Royal Engineers, attached to 44th Infantry Division, making Molotov cocktails – petrol bombs to throw at tanks – from beer bottles at Woodlands, Doncaster. One of the wooden crates holding the table up says 'Hammond's Bradford Brewery'. (War Office official photograph)

sorts, from his commander: 'Frequent representations are being made to higher authorities for better equipment and whilst the position is very unsatisfactory as far as I can ascertain we are receiving our fair share of any equipment issued.'

Shortages and mistakes, as the reply to Pochin said, were nothing personal, nor would they end soon. For every civilian with a military grievance, there was a military man with a grievance about the civilians – usually aired privately. General Dill, Chief of the Imperial General Staff, told his friend Archibald ('Archie') Wavell, commander in chief in the Middle East in a letter dated 6 June

> Of course we are taking great risks at home. We have plenty of men but having lost God knows how much equipment in Flanders we are left with uncommonly little at home. Guns of all kinds are particularly short not to mention tanks. And curiously enough one of our most serious shortages is SAA [small arms ammunition].

Here was one very senior man to another simply reporting how things stood, not blaming anyone. But generals seldom held back if they disliked their own civilians. Pownall, for instance, had sharp words in his diary concerning south Wales, after a September visit:

I was left with a very poor impression of the lower commanders in that part of the world. They behaved I believe as well as they know how to but they are a narrow-minded, quarrelsome, intriguing, petty-fogging people.

Pownall's prejudice against Wales may have stemmed from, or been reinforced by, a July meeting in the House of Commons with 30 'rather truculent members from Wales' and a famous but ageing Welsh politician: 'Lloyd George developed an attack on the Army for not using local talent and old war experience. ... So far as the LDV are concerned that is the sheerest nonsense.' Though Pownall had expressed the same complaint as Lloyd George in his diary a few weeks before.

So much for Ironside's wish for 'no council rows'. Alas, the truth was that the war's sudden turn for the worse prompted people to blame others. The vicar of Uttoxeter in Staffordshire, W.E. Charlton, in a sermon on the national day of prayer – Sunday 26 May, when the surrounded BEF certainly needed prayers – spoke of 'terrible failures' on the part of those they had trusted. He spoke of self-complacency, and underestimation of the enemy.

Rows were inevitable, even helpful if something better emerged. George Lindsey was deputy regional commissioner in Bristol. In a typed letter to Dill, Lindsay, a 1914–18 veteran of the Machine Gun Corps, said: 'Perhaps it is now too late. Hitler has forestalled me in this letter as he has forestalled many others.' By hand he wrote at the end, 'I know tank matters require investigation also. We only played at armoured war and those of us who were too insistent about it were considered fanatics. I trust that we shall not pay for it too dearly.'

As soon as anyone talked about having to 'pay' for things done wrong or not done in the past, politics came up. George Lane, the watch and clock repairer in Kidderminster, told his diary on 3 July: 'Chamberlain has given an interview to American journalists saying it is not true that he or any Conservatives want to start peace negotiations with Hitler which shows his "appeasement" policy is not forgotten … Judging by the Press and what one hears and thinks there is a big body of opinion to chuck them out.' As Lane wrote, might Chamberlain and his kind 'work a fast one on the Petain model?' Petain being the French general who had just taken office under the Germans.

General Sir Henry Pownall pictured in 1941. In the summer of 1940 he was trying to knock the Home Guard into shape – and keeping a diary recording his frustrations.

Some observers damned all politicians. After the French in mid-June decided not to defend Paris, one north London weekly newspaper's commentator, 'Augur', was shocked by the 'rottenness' of France's regime. However, Britain was not blameless, and he saw a lesson:'... the whole ruling class from right to left was united to get fat at the expense of the community. We too have allowed politicians to establish among themselves a sort of community the object of which is to cover each other's responsibility.' Did he have the Conservative MP who, like Ironside, appealed for 'no quarrels' – Churchill – in mind, for protecting his fellow Conservative Chamberlain?

OBSTACLES

While people were bickering, the military sought to build physical defences in a hurry. The chiefs of staff told the War Cabinet as early as 29 May that Germany might stabilise the front in France and seek to attack Britain. 'We are not satisfied from the military point of view that in the face of this danger the country as a whole has been sufficiently warned or adequately organised to meet the threat on which the fate of our land and empire may depend.' England was unready. The military advisers to the government warned of a new form of attack, a 'large fleet of fast motor boats' carrying 100 men each, crossing the North Sea in the dark and probably running up on the beaches.

> We have always held that the most hazardous phase of a combined operation is the actual landing of the men on the beach against opposition. Unless therefore we can ensure that the enemy is met on the beach by every possible form of defence: guns (within the limit of the numbers available), rifle fire, wire obstacles and demolitions, he may get that first and all important foothold on our territory which will enable large and heavier forces to be landed subsequently. We have ample evidence of the difficulty of dislodging the German once he has established himself on enemy soil.

Filey Bay in Yorkshire. By the end of 1940, two beach (static, second-rank) divisions and 4 Division were based in east Yorkshire and Lincolnshire.

Deal Pier from North Esplanade, and the strand and beach at Walmer. Regular troops were concentrated in the south-east where invasion was most likely to come.

The chiefs recommended that the country be warned and aroused to the 'imminent' danger. Labourers would have to put beaches in Yorkshire, East Anglia, the south-east, and south coast to Newhaven, in a state of defence.

In a memo to the War Cabinet dated 5 June, Eden made the work so far on home defence seem, at first glance, thorough. Every landing ground in the Metropolitan Area had been looked over, and 'many' made unusable. Work had started around ports. Preparations for demolitions of bridges on roads from ports from Aberdeenshire to Kent were 90 per cent completed. Road blocks were of 'any improvised material that is available on or near the site'.

Months of labour on obstacles was, according to the military later, often in vain, and needed re-doing. On 7 September, Lieutenant-General Auchinleck called much of the work 'too obvious'.

> It is necessary now to put this right without delay. The mere sight of a sandbag is enough to put an enemy on his guard. A good deal of the earlier work is not proof against rifle fire and is therefore an actual danger rather than a safeguard.

In Northamptonshire, Sir Hereward Wake sent out some sound advice – whether his men took any notice is another matter. Blocks had to go where they would hold up enemy traffic – for example, at a river, or a river bridge; 'no use in open space'. A block had to have a gap, to let through friendly traffic. As for when to set them up and man them, that would be when the enemy appeared or was reported nearby. As so often in 1940, at the very moment when the man on the spot most needed an order, the authorities gave up: 'There will probably be no time to refer to higher authority when the enemy lands so LDV commanders must act on their own responsibility remembering not to yield to panic and make blocks all over the place where no enemy are.'

Be prepared, and, in capital letters: 'DON'T PANIC', said the *Daily Express*, the largest-selling newspaper in Britain. Another newspaper advised the same:

> If your village is besieged there will be jobs for everyone, but whatever the job, there is a motto for man, woman, boy and girl. It is this; don't give in. don't lose your head. Don't panic. Remember that every moment gained in delaying the advance of the enemy helps your country.

These papers were only following the government's lead. A leaflet from the Ministry of Information, re-drafted after the War Cabinet went over it on 12 June, told the country: 'But think always of your country before you think of yourself.'

Were all people even obeying that basic appeal – to put their own interests aside, so that they did not hinder anyone, never mind doing something useful? It seems not. Harold Butler, the Reading regional commissioner, in an article on home defence, wrote: 'There are still some people who do not seem to realise that there is a war on or that they themselves are in any personal danger.' He was writing in late May about air raids, but some felt the same was true as invasion loomed. Weeks later the north London newspaper columnist 'Heathman' called for every able-bodied man aged 18 to 50 to enrol for war service of some kind at once. 'For too long have many of us taken this war lightly,' he argued.

EVACUATION

By early June – a good two weeks after Eden raised the LDV over the radio – it dawned on the government that they should have – in the words of a 3 June memorandum to the War Cabinet by the Ministry of Information – a 'campaign to prepare the public for invasion'. The information campaign would seek to calm the public. People had 'already observed defensive preparations being adopted and anxiety would be allayed if full warning and instructions were issued immediately'. An outline of a publicity campaign started with Churchill's 'fight them on the beaches' speech to MPs on 4 June.

On 5 June Sir Hugh Elles, described as chief of the civil defence operational staff, made a broadcast much-quoted in the following weeks, on how to behave in the event of invasion. He began by admitting a lot of 'rumour and speculation', especially in the eastern counties, about invasion. 'The danger of invasion is no new one.' Against Napoleon, and during the last war, 'very complete arrangements were made to face the threat of invasion both in the south east counties and in East England. That will be in the memory of many of you.' Stating the obvious, he repeated, 'no invasion took place'. What was the duty of the average man or woman? His answer: what would Germans like to see? As in Poland,

Holland, Belgium, and Norway; confusion, 'roads thronged with a procession of hapless refugees on foot and in vehicles'.

People should instead be alert; determined not to spread rumour. They should not block the roads, and not become fugitives. They should keep their 'head clear and mouth shut', stay put and sit tight.

Much of his advice foreshadowed a leaflet from the Ministry of Information, redrafted after a War Cabinet meeting on 12 June. It told people to be 'calm, quick and exact' and offered seven rules. Briefly: 'stay put', 'do not believe or spread rumours', 'keep watch and report anything suspicious'; do not give or tell a German anything; 'be ready to help military'; in factories and shops, organise some system now to resist a sudden attack; and 'think before you act'.

Elles waited until the end of his broadcast – no doubt on purpose, after soothing people and geeing them up – to slip in a jarring note, overturning all he had said so far. He addressed one group:

> As for some people moving from the coast inland, there was no reason they should not, unless they were in civil defence, post office, utilities, doctors, etc. Indeed it may be that for military reasons, that is to help the soldiers, the government will take steps later on to evacuate from certain places portions of the civilian population as a precautionary measure just as we have evacuated some of the schoolchildren.

The slogan 'stay put' at least had a ring to it, like the speech by a Sussex MP, Rear Admiral T.P.H. Beamish around the same time, to his Lewes constituents: '… any nation that is a refugee nation is a beaten nation; therefore to put it bluntly, stay put'.

Yet such tough talk was only half the story. Sir Hugh Elles had been at work on evacuating hundreds of thousands of people from enemy-facing coasts for a good three weeks. On 13 May – the day before Eden made his radio appeal – Will Spens, the Cambridge regional commissioner, wrote to Sir Hugh about the evacuation 'problem'. As those officials appreciated already, if parachutists landed, it was then too late, impossible, to evacuate. Suggested first was evacuation of children from some coastal towns. Proposed was a 'shuttle system' of trains to areas inland. Government heads of department covering home security, health, transport and food, met on the morning of 15 May to discuss evacuation of Lowestoft, Great Yarmouth and Harwich – towns in Spens' Cambridge region. The meeting heard that it would mean suspending normal trains on branches serving the towns evacuated. The civil servants worked fast. The Ministry of Transport sent a three-page typed memo the same day, saying that the railways could evacuate towns, given 24 hours' notice. They could clear Harwich and Felixstowe in 12 hours and Yarmouth and Lowestoft in 48.

According to the minutes of a meeting at 10 Downing Street, on Monday 10 June, Elles went over the possible evacuation of coast towns. Timetables were

Waterways on the coast at Great Yarmouth. Behind regular troops on the coast the defence of East Anglia was largely in the hands of Home Guards in each village.

arranged and preliminary work nearly finished. Then came discussion. The Prime Minister thought it not right to order evacuation 'at the present time'. The Commander in Chief Home Forces warned that the invasion of Norway had shown you could not rely on any attack warning. 'A small German force might easily establish itself in a coastal town and then it would be very difficult to dislodge them if the whole civilian population was in the houses and blocking up the roads.' In practice, too, it was 'quite impossible' to stop people from streaming out into roads and trying to get away from the area of a landing. Militarily, then, there was everything to be said for moving people in advance.

Set against that was the question of whether the danger so great that it was worth disrupting whole towns. The cabinet did decide to 'stimulate' voluntary evacuation of the East Anglia and Kent coastal towns of up to 60 per cent of the population, and make evacuation compulsory only when invasion was probable. On 20 June some nineteen coastal towns from Great Yarmouth to Hythe were ordered to *plan* compulsory evacuation. Police and fire, doctors and nurses, transport, food, and utility workers would remain until told by the regional commissioner. Evacuation would be by free trains each holding 800. Posters would tell people to take only one suitcase. There would be no press publicity, local or national. On 19 June the Minister of Home Security met the press. He explained that publicity in newspapers of evacuation plans would be 'undesirable' because it would alert the enemy, and might distract from the 'staying put' leaflet. Inevitably, such a major relocation had major stumbling blocks: for example, one of the towns, Southwold, did not have a train station.

The War Cabinet on 25 June agreed to the evacuation of 'useless mouths' from the east and south-east coast towns after 1 July. On 27 June the War Cabinet agreed not to have compulsory evacuation of the nineteen towns – for the present. Evacuation would be only be ordered as a military necessity in the face of imminent invasion.

Clacton-on-Sea from Pier

Two views of Clacton Pier in Essex. Tens of thousands of people including the author's mother left their homes on the east and south east coast from May 1940. Press publicity was forbidden.

In the event, many people needed no government prompt. Clacton-on-Sea in Essex had a May 1940 population estimated at 15,500. By 26 June some 4,000 townspeople had evacuated privately, compared with 2,200 by the 'aided scheme'. At the extreme, Broadstairs (May population 7,500) had seven evacuation trains and 5,500 – more than two-thirds – evacuated by 3 July. That day, the post office delivered a leaflet to the nineteen towns signed by Sir Auckland Geddes, the Tunbridge Wells regional commissioner, or Spens, in the Cambridge region. It began: 'The public throughout the country generally are being told to stay put in the event of invasion. For military reasons however it will be necessary to remove from this town all except those persons who have been especially instructed to stay.' Workers should stay for the present. Mothers, children, the aged and retired and unoccupied should leave. At the War Cabinet the same day, military chiefs spoke of many signs of attempts to invade the country in the near future. The military stressed the danger of delaying compulsory evacuation until too late. From the civilian side, the Home Secretary and Minister of Home Security added that voluntary evacuation was 'still being stimulated', and public opinion was 'already somewhat jumpy' and would become more so if evacuation became compulsory. And was compulsion necessary, if only a few coastal towns were likely to be attacked? The War Cabinet stuck by its 27 June decision not to compel people to leave.

Other people made their own minds up to move inland. One of the first towns to the west of those officially evacuated, Eastbourne in East Sussex, was only 40 miles from Hythe and hardly any less in danger of invasion. In late July the local press reported that 50,000 were still living in Eastbourne and that a 'small proportion of the population has disregarded the request to stay put'. The last census had put the population at 57,435. In truth, far more than the 'small' 7,000 may have left the town, given that seaside resorts usually fill in summer.

Certainly in late June the local press complained that 'during the last fortnight Eastbourne like many other towns has seen an exodus of residents who have decided to take an early summer holiday.' On several days, the railway station booking office was besieged by crowds, 'mostly of the wealthy class and many others well known in public life … demanding tickets for some place or other which it is fondly hoped will in the event of an enemy invasion provide them with a harbour of refuge'. The newspaper deplored 'mass hysteria as undignified as it is unjustified'. The paper may have been slow to notice or admit the 'exodus'. A month earlier, the daily paper in Cheltenham was reporting how town hotels, already crowded, were 'swamped with inquiries for accommodation by letter, telegram and telephone from people living on the south and east coasts who are anxious to get away.'

As in the Cabinet in London, public figures in Sussex disagreed whether sea-siders should stay. The Bishop of Chichester, at a meeting of clergy he called, asked for the withdrawal of all children, whose parents could arrange it; and for voluntary evacuation of the elderly, infirm, and all 'whose duty and business did not require them to remain'. The local press condemned what it called a 'scuttle and run policy' and, more self-interestedly, warned that wholesale evacuation would plunge the town into depression, ruining good businesses (including the newspaper one, presumably).

Some children – usually of the wealthy – were evacuated to Canada. Apart from the numbers who did sail, many more families thought it over. George Lane, the Kidderminster watch-maker, put in his diary on 26 June 'Scheme for evacuation to Dominions now started, children only, five to 16, taking names at the schools today. We cannot send Michael alone.' Public schoolboy W. Brian Carter was sent for by the headmaster one morning, 'who told me that my parents had decided to send me to Canada with my younger brother; as we were related to the Governor General, the Earl of Athlone, it had been planned for us to live in his palace … a car was waiting for me, but I refused to go. My parents were not at all pleased, having paid for the car.'

CHAPTER 3

THE BATTLE OF BEWDLEY, 30 JUNE 1940

Even in these enlightened days I believe there are still simple souls who can comfort themselves, when *in extremis*, with the thought that the chaps at the top know best …

Lieutenant-General Sir Frederick Morgan, *Peace and War: A Soldier's Life*, 1961

Every parent evacuating themselves or their children, every hilltop watcher, was expecting something to happen. False alarms were inevitable. As early as 19 May, Warwickshire newspapers reported a 'mild parachute alarm over a wide area' as a woman from Hillmorton, near Rugby, saw a strange object in the sky. Police and special constables searched the countryside and stopped traffic on the main London road. Nothing turned up. A rumour swept Northumberland of 30 parachute troops at Beal, on the coast by Holy Island. And on 5 June, the LDV of Claverley in Shropshire had a telephone report of a parachutist. Company commander Hornblower and two men commandeered a car and were on the spot before the landing of what turned out to be a barrage balloon.

On 2 July Northamptonshire LDV told units: 'False reports of enemy landings have been received lately, creating alarm and causing LDV and troops to turn out for nothing. No report can be ignored in case it proves correct.' The advice urged commanders to check who sent the report, and when.

At 6am on Wednesday 2 July a woman in the west Cumbrian pit village of Cleator heard knocking at the front door. A man was shouting, 'The Germans are behind Dent, keep your doors locked.' The woman was – so she told a court a few weeks later – a 'bit upset about it', and told her daughter. The daughter was startled and went to the mine to tell her husband and other men. They told her not to worry.

Police traced the rumour – it had gone round nearby Egremont too, that Germans had landed on a neighbouring fell – to a house in Cleator, and a 67-year-

The bridge over the River Severn at Bewdley.

old 'very deaf' shift hand. He had been knocking up people in the terraced street. He only wanted to warn people, the accused told police. The shift hand had heard the rumour on his walk to work at Egremont, two-and-a-half miles away. Defending the accused was his son who (like his brother) was a member of the LDV. The son told the court 'a grave emergency' had arisen – on 3 July (the court report did not explain the difference of a day; it may have been a misprint, or a sign of the general confusion that summer). The LDV heard that Germans were going to land at any minute. Before going on duty, the son told his father. In fact the alarm was meant for another town of the same name (near Liverpool). The father thought he was doing a good turn by warning people on his way to work.

Case dismissed. Though the father's and son's stories did not tally, the magistrates accepted that it was not a crime to spread the news. The summer's most notorious case of a false alarm sprang from the same dilemma. Anyone, soldier or civilian, could cry, in good faith, 'parachutist!'. The future of the nation might depend on a prompt and thorough response. Yet once a false alarm went out, how was anyone to disprove it? Without a way to halt the call-out, where might it end?

THE CALL-OUT

Geoff Knowles knew what he had to do when the church bells rang to tell of German invaders on Sunday 30 June. He rode his bicycle to the Midland Bank in Stourport-on-Severn, the headquarters of the town's LDV. The seventeen-year-old's job was to stand outside with his rifle.

> My uncle was the chief constable of Worcestershire; he had put into my safe-keeping a rifle which he used for rabbit-shooting; it was a .22. And having a rifle in those days made you something; I was a man with a box of ammunition and a means to fire the ammunition.

A few miles upriver in Bewdley that afternoon – witnesses agree the day was hot – Bert Bainton was returning from a weekend Scouts camp. He set off to start a night shift at 6pm

> … only to find that the soldiers and TA [Territorial Army] were running about all over the bloody place; we went into Bewdley and had a look; evidently the TA from Worcestershire was in Bewdley and they were about to mine the bridge each side to stop any Germans going over.

A couple of miles away, in Kidderminster, another young man, Leonard Burrows, was a member of the LDV.

> My sergeant, he was a barber in Kidderminster, he said, you better get your uniform and your rifle – I was fully equipped at the time … There was a yard where they kept some of the ammunition for the Home Guard and he gave me a clip of five bullets; he said, 'make them all count' … and we had to go over to Bewdley, we stopped there for a couple of hours, and we were waiting for the South Staffs [regular soldiers] to come.

In short, a corner of Worcestershire was mobilising to face an invader. So too, in smaller ways, were civilians. Baron Parkes was an eleven-year-old boy hay-making in the fields a few miles from Bewdley.

> Somebody just came and said, the Germans had landed at Bewdley; it's the only time we ever locked our door, day and night. When we went to bed that night, I took the four-ten [he laughed at the thought in 2006 – it was a small shotgun] with me – I don't know what good that would have done.

His future wife June, aged ten at the time, recalled only her worried father, a member of the LDV, standing, saying to his family, 'I shall have to go.' Her father did go – wearing a helmet tied with string instead of a proper strap, according to his daughter. Men like him, torn between home and a greater duty, set off to meet an unknown enemy.

THE INQUEST

It is a strange newspaper that has a front page story about something that did not happen. So it was in the Wolverhampton daily paper, the *Express & Star*, on Monday 1 July. 'No parachute troops landed in Midlands', it said. There was 'no truth in stories circulated over a wide area that either a German plane or German parachute troops landed anywhere in Midlands yesterday'. It was, rather, so the paper judged, a good example 'of how facts are misrepresented and material provided for rumour-mongering by indiscreet people'. In fact, near a Worcestershire village a British plane had flown very low, and witnesses thought that it had landed and reported it. The story was then 'variously embroidered', so the newspaper said.

The postwar history of the local Home Guard battalion gave better details of what it called, self-mockingly, the 'Battle of Bewdley'. Two men first gave the alarm to Bewdley police at 4pm on Sunday 30 June, who passed it to Bewdley's defence volunteers. The major in command sent messages to Stourport police and the nearest Army barracks. By 5pm enough LDV men gathered to screen Ribbesford Wood, in the country between Bewdley and Stourport, and to man road blocks. At 5.30pm, on LDV orders, Stourport church bells rang, the signal that invaders were in the vicinity. At 7pm a Bren gun carrier arrived at Bewdley from the barracks, and later two platoons with fixed bayonets (but unloaded rifles) searched the wood.

A motorist reported a second alarm at 11pm that at 5pm (why the hours in between?) he heard crackling of wood in a coppice. There was another search. At 1.35am, police sent a message that an armoured car of two enemies dressed as English officers had to be stopped at all costs. The final all-clear came at 4am. The battalion history added:

> Civilians thronged every point of military activity throughout the action; roads and bridges were so crowded that troop movements and road checks were virtually impossible. High Street, Stourport and Load Street, Bewdley were both solid with people and matters were made worse by the fact that in both places there were motor coach trips due to return.

At the time, the Bewdley LDV company owned five .303 rifles, shotguns, and .22 rifles.

There were two sides to the defenders' shortcomings at the 'Battle of Bewdley', one military, one civilian. The military responded absurdly late and weakly to the

St Anne's parish church tops Bewdley's main street leading to the river front and bridge.

first report of invaders. Had real paratroopers dropped, the presumably fit, armed and motivated men would have had time to gather, and the first British soldiers sent against the phantom invaders were, so it was claimed after, without bullets in their rifles. And civilians, far from doing what they could to aid the defenders, were getting in the way – just as refugees had hindered troops in France and Belgium in May 1940.

Witnesses, too, in old age spoke of 'uproar' (Geoff Knowles) in Stourport, and 'pandemonium' (Leonard Burrows) in Bewdley. Either there was a vacuum where there should have been command, or various potential commanders – LDV, police, Army, civil defence, and local government – confused each other, and passed on dubious warnings. Surely, if English officers were driving around in an armoured car, weren't they most likely to be English officers rather than enemies in disguise? The likes of Geoff Knowles did not to know the details, but they had eyes: 'Should I say we were a little bit like headless chickens, because nobody seemed quite [to know] who was in charge.'

The Saturday after the 'battle', the *Kidderminster Times* quoted Shropshire ARP controller and chief constable Major H.A. Golden.

The criminal in most of these cases has been hay, caught in small whirlwinds. Hay has been caught up and duly reported as parachutists as it dropped. It is quite proper to report things but people must make every endeavour to make certain of their facts before reporting and make certain of what they see.

Why did the 'battle' run its course after someone's original mistake? Why did the authorities take it so seriously, yet send men into possible combat with no bullets in their rifles? Civilians too were at fault: they 'thronged' (Geoff Knowles' word) Bewdley town centre, which would have been a first stop for invaders landing in the wooded hills nearby, seeking to secure a crossing of the River Severn.

The official warnings of the past few weeks to stay put did work, in that there is no criticism of civilians fleeing as refugees. Dorothy Scott was a local farmer's daughter.

> I was 21 at the time, and we were living in Buttonoak outside of Bewdley. It was a summer evening, we were having a ride on our bicycles, my sister, myself and a friend, and we were quite a long way towards Cleobury and turning to the left takes you out on to the Clows Top road. Well, all this incident happened after we left home, we had just gone out in summer dresses, nothing else with us. When we got to the crossroads, the road goes on up to Clows Top, there used to be a police station on the corner; they were out across the road, Home Guard, guns, all the rest of it. So of course we had to get off our cycles, they wanted to know where were our identity cards, where were our gas masks, and all this; we explained we had just gone out for a ride, we had nothing with us. After a while they let us go on; we rode on down and then you go down into Bewdley. Well, it used to be called Wells Cut; we had to turn left to ride back to Buttonoak. There they were again across the road, same procedure, out they come; we got past that lot. But the best of all was when we got towards Buttonoak, there were our local Home Guard doing exactly the same thing; they knew who we were; but I think it was just the fact it was the first occasion they had been told to put into practice what they had been training to do. They knew who we were but we had to go through the same grilling and eventually were allowed to go home. It was laughable really, but they were so serious.

There was a limit as to how well informed countryside residents such as Dorothy Scott could be.

> Living in the country, we didn't have electricity, and the only radio we had, you had to have batteries, two batteries, the one being charged, well, our parents used to go to Kidderminster market every Thursday which was shopping day and you bought your whole week's supply on that day. So there again, you couldn't use the radio very much, we were almost rationed as to what we could listen to on the radio.

The 'stay put' advice backfired because civilians were in the way, whether going about their business, or out of sheer curiosity. Why? We can guess that civilians, not hearing any gunfire, took the military call-out as an unthreatening, even entertaining, false alarm.

Or were the crowds in Stourport and Bewdley – that could have hindered fighting men – merely a testament to the need for news, to make sense of danger? Given that the authorities were silent, or confused, people resorted to word of mouth, and, as Geoff Knowles pointed out, 'word spreads very rapidly through a small town.' And thanks to the mass recruitment of civilians as first aiders, air raid wardens and LDV men, most people knew someone mobilised that Sunday afternoon. 'Then it was like a Bank Holiday Monday, there were hundreds of people thronging around. People turned out, I suppose, for the say so of the thing … looking to see what they could see.'

Some of the people not supposed to be on the streets after the bells rang for invasion were there only because their usual Sunday work or play took them there. Buses from Birmingham still take summer Sunday and bank holiday day-trippers through Bewdley. Harry Bamfield and his friends were canoeing fanatics. They heard the bells and 'wondered what the hell was going on', Harry recalled in 2006. The boys put their canoes away and picked up their bicycles, as usual, near the bridge at Bewdley. 'When we went over the other side of the bridge, we were pulled over, we had no identity card … There was no getting over it [the bridge] either way.'

Eventually the guards let the boys go, told them to carry their identity cards with them next time; and to go home. 'But when we got out to [nearby] Catchems End there was another lot out.' The boys said they had already been stopped at Bewdley Bridge, and again the guards told them to go home. Harry Bamfield did go home. But what of the guards who were duty-bound not to go home until told to, early the next morning? Geoff Knowles remembered 'there was appre-hension, because people didn't know what was happening, and if nobody tells you anything, you are a little bit at sea.' Leonard Burrows found the experience 'very unpleasant, actually, it was frightening. It frightened us all. It was a load of baloney in the end, but it wasn't at the time.'

OTHER ALARMS

Few knew about the 'Battle of Bewdley' beyond the district. And while there was no sign of any military or civil defence authority wanting to get to the bottom of the affair to learn lessons, it does show an uncomfortable truth: for all the planning and publicity, when something does happen, people respond in unexpected ways, or not at all. The authorities would have to do some quick thinking.

Sir Hereward Wake sent a letter on 3 June, 'Copies to be given to all company and section leaders to read to their men'. After asking men inevitably for their patience about equipment they lacked, he turned from his men's morale to everyone else's.

> The LDV must help to prevent alarm among the population. We must be on our guard, but keep calm. Most of the stories about spies and so on are absurd and untrue. Remember that they are spread by the enemy to try and create a panic. We may have hard times but we are going to win this war.

Bewdley was only the most spectacular invasion false alarm of the summer, as jitters persisted. One corner of Staffordshire alone had several reports of parachutists landing in a LDV battalion area. Each time, the Burton-on-Trent LDV turned out. One report was of parachutists at Sinai, above the town; troops set off from three directions and nearly fought each other. It turned out the witness had mistaken wind lifting and dropping hay in the fields for Germans, the same as in Bewdley.

Somerset's Chief Constable, circulating a report in May 1941, called for care in verifying reports about parachutists.

> During last summer and autumn reports were FREQUENTLY received here [at Taunton police headquarters] of parachutes being seen and after much investigation and the occupying of the time of many police officers and the military the incidents were traced to such causes as eddies of wind taking up hay, peculiar formations of cloud and smoke, puffs from gunfire and drifting barrage balloons.

Syd Bailey wrote many years later:

> In 1940 I was a probationary police constable in Wolverhampton. One evening I was instructed to meet a police car, and I was then driven with three other officers towards Penn – where German parachutists were reported to have landed. Heavily armed with truncheons and whistles (plus handcuffs) we then set out to search for the enemy. What we were supposed to do when we found them was not made clear to us. What a heavily-armed German force would make of a welcoming committee of four policemen looking like the chorus in 'The Pirates of Penzance' was anybody's guess – but the whole business turned out to be a false alarm so the problem never had to be resolved.

Confusing things further, opinions differed on how to react to parachutists. Should you wait and ambush them, or rush to meet them as they landed, when they might be winded and vulnerable? The LDV training instruction number

Seated at the dining table with his wife, a sergeant of the Dorking Home Guard in Surrey gives his Tommy gun a final polish before leaving home to go on parade. While it's a wonderful scene that contrasts the domestic with the military, it's doubtful, once again, whether many (if any) 1940 Home Guards had such a sophisticated weapon. (War Office official photograph by Len Puttnam)

two was sure of one thing; the defenders needed the 'active and collective co-operation of the population'.

North of Northampton, on 20 August, the population certainly co-operated – all too actively. Letters after the event tell the story – one by Sir Hereward Wake dated 27 August, to Major Falkner, Brixworth Home Guard battalion commander, after a report by the Lamport company commander, John Houison-Crawford.

Houison-Crawford, of the nearby village of Chapel Brampton, reported on a notelet how he heard by phone at 6.55pm of a parachute. Unfortunately, the acting platoon commander, one down the chain of command, was away at the time. A more junior section commander, Mr Holmwood, took the original call. Houison-Crawford recalled: 'The report though substantiated by a number of witnesses was not very specific in that no-one had reported seeing a man on a parachute and by the time I enquired this point the informants had all gone off to look for the parachute.'

Lamport guards told the neighbouring village of Maidwell, and Houison-Crawford told Northampton. Another village called, to send a few men to where the parachute had been seen, at Short Wood. 'When I arrived at Lamport at 7.15pm no-one was to be found except Mr Holmwood ... all the rest of the platoon who could be collected had gone off in cars to Short Wood.' Even when

Houison-Crawford arrived at the wood, no-one was to be found. One of the platoon returned to report that another village Home Guard had told him the parachute was a barrage balloon that had come down.

Perhaps trying to avoid a telling-off from his superiors, Houison-Crawford laid down four lessons, covering everything about the event that never happened: 'importance of clear specific report', 'someone in authority to give orders', 'some scheme for each platoon to search properly rather than indiscriminate searching', and the need to stress to the public 'that they should stay put' … as the population of Lamport flocked out, children and all, to Short Wood.'

Sir Hereward Wake commented (by hand) on Crawford's report

> The important thing arising is the fact that the Home Guard section (accompanied by the inhabitants) all left the village and went off to search for one parachute. My God what a lot of spoon-feeding these chaps require. I will mention it in my next instructions. Meanwhile tell Crawford to stop such goings on. An empty parachute too.

On the left side of the paper, because he had run out of room, Sir Hereward – ever the stickler – wrote: 'Do ask Crawford to use foolscap.'

MIDSUMMER GUESSING

With the benefit of hindsight, we can see that the middle of the summer was a time of waiting and guessing, played on by enemy propaganda. As late as 14 September in an interview with George Bernard Shaw, the *Daily Express* asked him if he thought Hitler was going to invade Britain. Shaw replied with Shavian wit (or an 84-year-old's temper): 'How do I know? How does anybody know?'

He had plenty of company. George Lane entered in his diary on 12 July, 'The much awaited invasion has not materialised yet. Perhaps they hope to cripple our Navy and shipping and ports first. I suppose he will try it when he is good and ready.' On 16 July he wrote 'All comparatively quiet but the Axis press says Britain has had its last quiet weekend. We shall see.' As we know now, the Luftwaffe broke the quiet by opening the Battle of Britain against the RAF, rather than a parachutist or sea invasion, but at the time the British were not to know. In his letter of 18 July to Wavell in Egypt, Dill said he was even less inclined than usual to make prophecies. 'It looks as though Hitler is not going to launch a blitzkrieg on this country within the next few days. Iceland and Ireland appear in more immediate danger.'

As weeks passed, for all the nagging frustrations about a lack of rifles and ammunition, a more intangible need was emerging, as shown up by the farcical rushes to suspected parachutists around the shires. How did commanders communicate the most basic orders to their men, such as when to turn out, and

A 'fighting column' from the South Wales Borderers man their motorcycles, parked in a suburban street in Bootle, Liverpool. Like so many photos of the time, this scene made good, misleading propaganda – few soldiers were this well equipped. (War Office official photograph, 16 August 1940)

where to go? And if the men were volunteers, how could you order them to do anything they did not like, although it might make military sense?

WHAT'S IN A NAME?

By the end of July, on the orders of Churchill, the LDV had its name changed to Home Guard. Pownall, writing in his diary on 29 July, after a tour of western England, was haughty:

> The change of title from LDV to Home Guard is purely Winstonian and is a great nuisance. He could have well left things alone. But Home Guard rolls better off the tongue and makes a better headline.

King George VI talking to a member of the Home Guard during an inspection in Kent. Though the name 'Local Defence Volunteers' had gone a few weeks before, the man still has an LDV armband. (War Office official photograph, 10 August 1940)

While the name Home Guard stuck, some claimed to prefer the old one. A. J. Parkes, the opinionated Tettenhall, Staffordshire battalion commander, claimed to be attached to the old name. 'The change was significant. We were becoming more like soldiers and the old free and easy spirit was in consequence to some extent militarised.'

It might seem strange that the commander of a defence force should feel it a blow to become more 'militarised'. The fading of their early unregimented enthusiasm was symbolised by the new name imposed on them from the top. The same was happening in tactics – the ways they planned to fight, ways they had not dreamed of a few weeks before.

CHAPTER 4

TACTICS

The soldier's speculative faculty can be stilled by drilling.
Carlyle, *The French Revolution*

On Saturday 1 June, farmer Albert Arkell was in a carpenter's shop in Bibury in the Cotswolds, when Cecil Large, a village game keeper, called in. Large asked Arkell, as one LDV member to another, whether he had seen anything on an early morning patrol. Arkell said no, adding, 'You won't get me out on a wild-goose chase like that again – the thing wants reorganising.' Large replied, 'You are one of the kind of men Hitler would like to have about.'

No doubt incensed, Arkell asked Large what he did in the last war. Large answered by giving Arkell a black eye, which was how the story came to Fairford court and in the local paper a fortnight later. Arkell told magistrates he resigned from the LDV after the fisticuffs. He had been on patrol for the first time from 3.30am to 6am, under Large's command. Large, defending himself, told the court that when the First World War broke out he was only thirteen – clearly Arkell's jibe had got to him. Though Large claimed Arkell faced up to him, Large was fined £1 for assault. While it was no business of the court to ask, we can presume that Arkell had a grudge against a (younger) man of lower social rank in command of him; alternatively, Arkell was short-tempered after a sleepless night for no purpose. Whatever the reason for the argument, this story shows that the choices made by commanders, the demands on their men – in a words, their tactics – were not, as in the Army, simply things the soldiers had to lump. Everyone wanted to do a good job, but what did that mean?

In the summer of 1940, the defenders did not know how much time they could count on for training: days, weeks or the whole summer? Certainly not the months, even years, it might take to make a first-rate soldier. According to Fred Barratt, the Staffordshire Home Guard man, a Major Adie told him 'Our aim is to

Fred Barratt and fellow volunteers at practice.

slow them up until heavier units are called up. We are practically a suicide force. Knock one or two out before they know where we are.'

Fred's platoon, based on a Black Country factory, did not have many fixed defences: 'We had one or two sandbagged emplacements by the brook and the side of the bridge.' Platoon headquarters was a farm. 'Really, the winners are those the fastest to learn, the more you think about it!'

FIGHTING TALK

For a country that had lost its continental allies, it was striking how Britain spoke of returning to the offensive; though men may have spoken so aggressively because anything more than talk was not feasible. In one of the many Home Guard handbooks printed that summer, Lieutenant-Colonel Sir Thomas Moore MP in a foreword dated 29 July 1940 wrote of the strategy for the remainder of the war, ending with landing an expeditionary force on the continent to defeat the enemy in the field. Meanwhile, 'The Home Guard will become the defenders of these islands.' The job? 'To defend our country if necessary to the last man'. The

Fig. 8—USE OF COVER

Shooting round cover. The arm, not the rifle, should rest against the side of the cover, a firm grip being maintained. There is no undue exposure

Fig. 5.—THE LOADING POSITION

Note particularly that eyes are fixed on the mark. Finger is not on the trigger, even though loading has been finished. The rifle is held so that it can easily be brought into the aiming position

Fig. 2.—THE STANDING POSITION

The points to be noted are : a firm balanced base for the body, good grip with both hands, head well back from the cocking-piece, left forearm under rifle. The right arm need not be quite so high as is here shown

THE PRONE POSITION

The points to be noted are : Head well back from cocking-piece, good grip with both hands, elbows not too far apart, stomach and legs flat on the ground, legs well apart

Illustrations from the fourth edition (July 1940) 'Textbook for Local Defence Volunteers', entitled *Rifle Training for War* by Captain Ernest H. Robinson. These and other drawings showed the immaculate English gentleman in suit and tie wearing a tin helmet and aiming his rifle behind cover, loading, aiming while standing and aiming in the prone position.

John Langdon-Davies, an English journalist who reported on the Spanish Civil War. He seized the moment in 1940 and wrote a string of books and newspaper columns about the Home Guard.

handbook's author, Alfred Kerr, took up this theme at once. Every foot of the country should be covered 'by men trained and ready to resist even to the death if necessary.'

Men, whether organising themselves, writing handbooks to educate others, reading and taking notes, talking amongst themselves or on formal occasions, were forming a new organisation, albeit for a purpose with plenty of historical precedence, for example in the wars against Napoleon. As the revolutionary organisers of new French armies of the 1790s found, talking and writing did not put uniforms on backs or rifles on shoulders; nor did it teach men how to work with their fellows, either at drill or in the confusion and noise of battle. The writers, such as Kerr, knew this too. '[The] whole organisation and training' of the Home Guard was, as he put it politely, 'in an embryo stage of development.'

Development into what? 'Marlborough, Wellington, Haig have all told us that armies cannot be improvised in a moment. We never remember this,' wrote Lilias Bathurst, wife of the seventh Earl, to her local Cirencester newspaper, in the first days of the LDV. She was unhelpful, but right.

How to teach men, when everyone was feeling their way? It is easy to forget how daring it was in 1940 to launch a national body, the LDV, over the radio. As always, someone grabbed the opportunity. John Langdon-Davies arguably was the man who jumped most spectacularly and profitably onto the Home Guard bandwagon. In the winter of 1940–1 the author and journalist spoke to tens of thousands of men at mass meetings around the country. He and others, wise to the ways of newspapers, created a loop; they wrote for a paper, collected articles as books, talked to audiences (the venues advertised beforehand in the newspaper) and, from questions and discussions with those attending, gathered more material for speeches and newspaper articles. Lasngdon-Davies was awarded an MBE for services to the Home Guard.

DEBATE

The Army had the same debate, partly in public, that retired officers were having in print. Before Dunkirk was surrounded, Major-General Sir Charles Gwynn was writing in the *Daily Telegraph* of the enemy's advance at 'amazing speed'. Serving officers, too, sought answers in private. As Dill, chief of the imperial general staff, wrote to 'Archie' Wavell, commander in chief Middle East on 18 July: 'The Army at home is still woefully short of training. Far too much time is spent in making

Norman Corbett in RAF uniform. Earlier in 1940 he was one of the guards of his Darlaston, West Midlands factory, each given a rifle with two bullets.

defences and guarding beaches etc but I hope that things in that respect will greatly improve.' Dill wanted to get a committee together on the Army of the future, and asked Wavell for his 'loose thoughts'.

The danger was that each little unit would try to re-invent the wheel. It was difficult, but not impossible, to separate a tactical idea from someone's political and general outlook. Conservatives tended to be conventional, left-wingers tended to embrace radical new ways of war. Were Home Guards meant to keep the peace and leave the fighting to regular soldiers, or would everyone have a go, alone? Were they guerrillas, best doing ambushes, or should they strive to be like the main army? Would they stick to the rifle and bayonet for normal combat, or trust in knives, petrol bombs and booby-traps, for street and irregular fighting? Not being able to arm the Home Guard properly, or at all, was the authorities' secret shame of 1940 – and beyond. As late as June 1941, the Army admitted that about 666,000 of the one million Home Guards had no personal weapons.

The men on the receiving end of such shortages saw how things stood. Norman Corbett was a factory LDV at the Black Country steel foundry F.H. Lloyd in Darlaston in 1940–1, until he volunteered for the Royal Air Force.

It was a bit farcical at times. When we went on duty at the gates we only used to be issued with two bullets because everything was scarce. Plus we were inexperienced and might have done damage if we had let them off. You had to sign [for the bullets] and when your guard was over, two hours on and four hours off, you used to have to hand the bullets in again, so that somebody else could have them.

The factory had 'three or four rifles' and made its own dummy guns.

REALITY

A revealing trio of letters show how thin the defence was on one stretch of south Devon and Dorset beach. The LDV commander in Seaton, a Lieutenant-Colonel Lethbridge, wrote to Ismay on 1 July that beyond the 50th Division, only a battalion of infantry, based at Exmouth, stood between Lyme Regis and Exmouth (about 30 miles of coastline). At Seaton was one company of 'old soldiers' for defence of an internment camp, now closed. Otherwise there was only the LDV with 'a few rifles and shotguns'.

> On Sunday we began to make anti-tank defence barriers on the esplanade and the same is being done at Sidmouth, Budleigh Salterton and intervening small beaches. The whole population has been out here digging shingle to help on the work. Behind this the necessary road blocks are to be established but apart from LDV and the few men Exmouth can spare there is nothing. I have discussed this matter with Colonel Rohde, the CO at Exmouth and with the camp commandant here and we are all of the same opinion.

Namely, there was a gap, but practically no help within an hour by road. (So much for mobile reserves.)

On 6 July Ismay wrote from the War Cabinet Office to Brigadier Jack Swayne, assistant chief of general staff. Ismay said he had had a letter from a friend in the LDV at Seaton, who had written that there were no troops between Lyme Regis and Exmouth.

> I know only too well how great are the calls upon your resources and I have no doubt you have fully appreciated the above facts. I nevertheless thought it right to draw attention to them. You can of course put this letter in the waste paper basket and I shall certainly not expect any reply.

The next day Ismay, using his nickname 'Pug', answered Lethbridge – they were members of the United Services Club in Pall Mall, and wrote to each other via that address – with sympathy.

> I am very much afraid that your particular beaches are not the only ones on which the strength of the defensive forces is not as great as its holders could wish. The country is a mass of beaches each one more desirable than the last and we have to rely very largely on defeating whatever may succeed in landing by using strong mobile reserves!

Meanwhile, a dozen miles to the other, east side of Lyme Regis, the 6th Durham Light Infantry (DLI) by 2 July was dug in at the village of Litton Cheney, between

A car negotiates a barricade of concrete blocks on the road between Warnham and Horsham, Surrey. Would German tanks or paratroopers have gone around the obstacles in a similar fashion? (War Office official photograph, 26 June 1940)

A car passes a sandbagged barricade on the A23 road from London, near Brighton. The soldier beside the stop-go sign was plain enough by day, but after dark, drivers could be, and were, shot at by nervous guards. (War Office official photograph, 26 June 1940)

Bridport and Dorchester, alongside LDV posts. A and B Companies each held about one mile of beach, between Burton Bradistock and Portisham. The advanced battalion headquarters was by a tumulus to the south of the village of Swyre, at The Knoll. This was Thomas Hardy country – indeed the Hardy monument on the road to the author's home town of Dorchester lay on the battalion's boundary line. Compared with the trenches of the First World War, the Durham battalion was spread impossibly thinly. A division would have held the equivalent of couple of miles of trenches in 1914–18.

Nor did the battalion have weapons or defences to make up for lack of numbers; quite the opposite. Its first 'operational instruction' dated 4 July read: 'In case of attack sentries will fire two shots in rapid succession.' In other words, the defenders did not yet have Verey pistols to fire warning lights. All posts as far as possible were to be 'wired around' and linked with crawl trenches. Intentional gaps would 'shepherd' any penetrating enemy into areas covered by machine-

Men of the Australian Imperial Force stage a cricket match, July 1940.

guns. Dummy pillboxes would stand every 100 yards. An anti-tank ditch would be dug, 'under civilian arrangement'. The local LDV – two companies, at Burton Bradstock and Winterbourne – in an emergency would defend road blocks and their villages; round up parachutists with the DLI; and destroy petrol supplies ('a complete list of petrol tanks in the area will be issued later').

The battalion was still working out its role in its third such instruction, dated 15 July. Six places were named where tanks could 'probably' thrust inland. To stop them the unit had 950 mines; a 'tank hunting platoon' with another 100 mines; the ditch (but even so some tanks would get across, the document admitted) and six-pounder guns ('these should arrive shortly'). The ultimate policy was 'to cover closely with mines the whole of the front where tanks could cross'. Meanwhile mines were scarce.

On a larger scale, in September 1940, 50th Division – based at Blandford, part of Montgomery's 5 Corps – was still covering the coast from Lyme Regis to Poole, about 45 miles by road. A division in France in 1914–18, and 1939–40, had a tenth or less of front to cover.

You could argue that coastal infantry units needed only to stand and fight. If any units needed equipping and training, they were the mobile reserves which, as Ismay and others said, would have the most demanding task. The reserves would drive to where the enemy was most threatening, and out-fight him –for the reserve to merely block the invader would only postpone defeat. Such a

Troops of the 2nd Australian Imperial Force on the quayside after disembarking at Gourock in Scotland. (War Office official photograph, 17 June 1940)

reserve was the 'Australian Striking Force', part of Salisbury-based Southern Command. A conference on 26 July agreed the Australians' role would be to destroy airborne troops landing on Salisbury Plain and in the South Midland area to the north.

As a result, Australian detachments protecting Andover and Middle Wallop aerodromes were withdrawn the next day. Australians, with a high reputation as can-do infantrymen from 1914–18, would have motor coaches as transport. The force needed 73; of those, 60 would each carry 20 men, the rest ferry staff and equipment, but as late as 14 September only 30 vehicles were available. If extra coaches were not found from outside sources, 'the force would have to be moved by relays', which would mean barely half the force would be mobile at a time. Even according to its order of battle, SPA (Salisbury Plain Area) Striking Force spread over miles. Its headquarters was in a field near Potterne police station, while detachments were more than 20 miles apart as the crow flew, at Chisleton, Burbage, Salisbury race course, Teffont, Manor House, Seend, Kington Langley, and a central reserve at Market Lavington. They might have to drive 60 miles in any direction to fight parachutists. Their artillery batteries had guns as heavy as 25-pounders, but not enough quads to pull ammunition trailers, and lorries would have to carry the rest of the front line ammunition.

Such shortages had lasted all summer, because a vehicle survey dated 31 July found the Australians short of every vehicle except cars. They had half

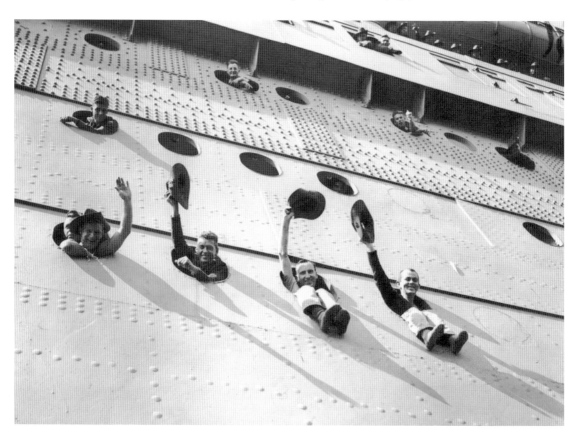

Troops of the 2nd Australian Imperial Force wave from portholes as their troopship docks at Gourock on the Clyde. (War Office official photograph, 19 June 1940)

A machine-gun battalion moves out of camp. In truth the Australians, like the rest of the regular Army in England in the summer of 1940, were short of motor transport and most other equipment.

An Australian infantryman with an anti-tank rifle behind cover, August 1940.

of the motorcycles they wanted, and of the machine-gun battalion, only one company was really mobile. Of the requisitioned transport, half was 'junk' and half could be made serviceable by the Australians working in Army workshops at Tidworth and Bulford. Some types of vehicle were not satisfactory, just light vans. The Australians wanted eight per battalion of the 30 cwt type; they had two.

BAYONET BELIEVERS

Although the average Home Guard infantryman had at best only a personal firearm, commentators could not agree on how he should fight with what little he had. For a commentator and a First World War veteran open to modern ideas like John Brophy, the bayonet was 'essentially a weapon for sentries and night patrols', or for searching houses in street fighting. In some places a bayonet charge as in 1914 (or 1815) was still all the rage. A.E. Anslow, a former Home Guard platoon sergeant at Seighford, near Stafford, recalled later.

A platoon of the Royal Scots Fusiliers stage a bayonet charge on an unidentified east coast beach. This looked stirring but was purely a stunt for the camera. (War Office official photograph by Len Puttnam, 19 July 1940)

Periodically we should be notified of a mock attack by a neighbouring unit, the exercise would be at a weekend, usually Sunday, and we would discuss plans to oppose them. We were always ready for them but somehow these exercises were far from realistic. Enemy units would be engaged as they advanced in open formation irrespective of any danger ahead. To me this was all wrong, if it happened on active service they certainly would have been destroyed long before their objective had been reached. Our orders were to fire and retreat, fire and retreat. We utilised all available cover as far as nature provided and it really was ridiculous to keep advancing in the face of such opposition. To my mind this sort of exercise was not very satisfactory and totally inconclusive; I was sometimes annoyed at this play-acting especially as the umpires and officers never held any discussion on the results or merits of the action.

A CSM (Company Sergeant Major) Jock Cameron recalled in the Hove Home Guard magazine how in LDV days

Many members did their damndest to discourage me in training the lads on how to use the bayonet. According to them the Bayonet was primitive and a thing of the past. At least I knew that Bayonet fighting keyed a man up, taught him to throw his rifle about, gave him added confidence and last but not least was a relaxation from the boring if very necessary musketry and squad drill.

In other words, using the bayonet at least made the civilian-soldier more warlike. Such a defence of the *arme blanche* is not to be dismissed out of hand. Writing in early 1941, Cameron was able to add triumphantly that the Greeks, and the Australians in Libya, had used the bayonet against the Italians, to (as he put it) 'mop the wops up'.

STATIC OR MOBILE?

Talking tactically, the choice for Home Guards in a town or group of villages was between static or mobile. Each had its merits, and ideally an overall defence would include both. Even the very highest commanders argued over the right balance between static, lesser-trained and equipped soldiers who would at best merely halt the invader, and mobile motorised troops who with more training would have the role of defeating the enemy. According to the record of a 6 August 1940 meeting between Alan Brooke, CiC Home Forces, and various generals,

> C in C stated that mobile offensive action must be the basis of our defence. The idea of linear defence must be stamped out; what is required to meet the dual threat of seaborne and airborne attack is all-round defence in depth with the maximum number of troops trained and disposed for a rapid counter-offensive. Armoured formations should be employed in the van of the attack with the object of creating a situation which could be exploited by motorised infantry.

Brooke set out what he called 'most serious difficulties': a higher standard of motor mobility was required, and 'higher foot mobility' – that is, fitter infantrymen. And – more evidence that training, role, tactics and weapons were interdependent – Brooke called for 'bolder moves' in training.

Alert generals agreed. Montgomery took over from Auchinleck at 5 Corps on 22 July. In one of his first operational instructions on 27 July, he said that 'Working on defences alone will not produce fighting efficiency.' The challenge was to maintain balance between defence work – the army was after all digging a new front line – training and recreation.

There was no point in Brooke or anyone else relying on a mobile defence, if the static part of the defence did not do its bit. Home Guards would tend to be static, if only because they would not know where else to go. Enthusiasts such as Sir Hereward Wake in Northampton urged the LDV in towns to provide 'flying columns', or to be exact, troops in lorries, ready at short notice to reinforce local units 'within say about ten miles'. It is doubtful if anything came of this. What local commander would feel comfortable sending his most experienced men miles away? In any case there were never enough men to go around.

Defence was about the art of the possible. H. V. Morton, the Hampshire platoon commander told Colonel Charteris, his Alton company commander, in a June letter about the problem of road messengers. 'We have all been warned not to send men wandering about the country at night in case they are shot up by the mobile column.' If the telephone went dead, the Home Guards would have to send messengers by road. 'As all my men are agricultural labourers with enormous families, I do not feel inclined to take upon myself the risk of asking them

Men of 7th Battalion, the Green Howards among the sand dunes at Sandbanks, near Poole in Dorset. This is probably how the soldiers would have met the invaders – only much more thinly spread. (War Office official photograph, 31 July 1940)

to commit suicide.' Anyone carrying a message in the dark risked being mistaken for an enemy and shot at.

Morton called on the authorities to make some lanes to the nearest towns of Bordon and Aldershot safe to send cars or cyclists – 'having been on duty at night with my men and having heard their questions and problems, most of them extremely shrewd and sensible'. Morton wanted to know where he stood. But, Morton either did not consider or did not bother asking, would invaders oblige by keeping off those 'recognised' roads? As it was asking too much of Home Guards to dash after the invaders, and there were not enough troops to make reserve lines, the defence soon came to hinge on 'nodal' or 'focal' points inland, at main towns, often river crossings.

As a January 1941 general staff note argued, the enemy's main objective would be the centre of government in London. Hence Britain would defend in depth inland, behind the beaches. The Army saw complications. Because they were not fighting in an empty desert or jungle, but in their own country, civilians would get in the way. During enemy bombing, the army already found it difficult keeping civilians 'out of our pillboxes owing to lack of sufficient civilian shelters'. The general staff hinted that the civil authorities would agree to do something about rationing, fire fighting and casualty rescue and so on, in a nodal point, but would not actually do anything beforehand, because to do something would cost money and resources.

Eventually the issue – who would do what if the enemy reached a town – had to go to a higher level. Sir Auckland Geddes, regional commissioner for the Tunbridge Wells-based 12 region, covering the south-east, went on a tour of Kent fortresses and nodal points in October 1940. Sussex had the same treatment in early 1941. The work needed to prepare whole south coastal counties against an invasion was daunting. In November 1940, Tenterden (described as an 'important road venue') would 'burn like match board if bombed', the general staff warned. The town had inadequate fire fighting and little water, and yet was 'packed' with civilians.

The commanders evolving the tactics were proceeding by trial and error. For the average volunteer, that meant digging more trenches. The Home Guard historian in Abingdon:

> Brasshats appeared, disapproved of siting of most of them [the trenches] and ordered last night's sweated labour to be done all over again, 'tonight – tomorrow may be too late'. A day or two later a 'high up' with other ideas disapproved of the new siting.

FAITH IN BRICKS

Given the hurry to be ready, and the lack of weapons, let alone modern weapons that would match the Germans', the defenders knew that they could not be strong enough everywhere. One answer from the authorities – who were the ones with the budget to spend – was to build defences, in the hope that walls and trenches would do the work of some defenders, besides protecting them.

The Army did its best to control the sudden and massive contract work. On 2 July Brigadier Ian Thomson, commander of 26th Infantry Brigade based in northern Scotland, complained in a letter to Inverness barracks that a contractor – also named Thomson – had been away from Wick where he was supposed to be building a pillbox at Wick aerodrome. The Brigadier complained of 'inferior' workmanship, and doubted if the pillbox would be bullet-proof. He asked about a contractor for a 'most urgent' pillbox for Castletown, and asked Royal Engineers Captain Stevenson to visit works more frequently. The next day a Royal Engineers major defended himself and Stevenson in a return letter. It was difficult to get bricks or concrete blocks for all emergency work. Kilns at Brora, the main source for the north, were working day and night. The contractor had been absent from Wick to meet another major about a Thurso transport camp contract. Summing up, not that reassuringly, Stevenson was satisfied the Wick workmanship was 'as bullet-proof as 18-inch brick work can be'.

The irregulars mocked such faith in bricks and concrete. As Canadian-born and Ohio-raised Bert 'Yank' Levy, the guerrilla warfare teacher at Tom

Concrete road barriers in Cheriton, Kent. In the background, an East Kent Bus shelter converted into a pillbox. Note the old-fashioned dustbin as pushed by a street cleaner, on the left. Life had to go on. The sign on the right says 'Air raid shelter 200 yards'. (War Office official photograph by Len Puttnam, 10 July 1940)

A pillbox south of Frinton-on-Sea, and another looking north to the previous box, with railings added since the war.

Wintringham's school, The Osterley Park School for the Home Guard Training Centre, wrote: 'The serious thing to do in modern war if we are to judge from the efforts of officialdom is to sit in a blockhouse that is the most obvious feature of any landscape and get what is coming to you.' A sentiment also expressed in different words by General George S Patton: 'Fixed fortifications are monuments to man's stupidity.'

The unpleasant truth was that whatever they did, the defenders could not be strong everywhere. On the south coast, Montgomery wrote in December 1940:

The corps commander [Montgomery] has noticed that there are a great many cases of undue dispersion within platoons in the case of battalions holding the coastline. The very long frontages which have to be held have led to a desire to defend every possible landing place, and this has led to excessive dispersion. But isolated section posts have no possible hope of survival in the modern battle. We have got to accept risks and concentrate our platoons and when necessary our companies in strong well-wired localities capable of all round defence and capable of holding out till our reserves get into action. There may often be gaps between localities that cannot be avoided when holding long fronts. These gaps must be patrolled, particularly in foggy weather.

DRILL OR INITIATIVE

Meanwhile, the average soldier knew little and cared less about tactics. John Kenneally in his war memoir – he later won a Victoria Cross in North Africa – took only a page to describe his summer of 1940. He was one man in a Lewis gun team defending an airfield in Essex – 'We lay on our backs getting suntans and watched the proceedings in the sky.' He manned road blocks, helped to build anti-tank traps and attended anti-tank courses. 'There have been millions of words written about the Battle of Britain but not many by an ordinary soldier who had a ringside seat,' he wrote. Ironically the publisher who reprinted the memoir after Kenneally's death edited much of the 1940 part out. There lay an insight; the ordinary soldier had little to say because he had little to do but watch, and at most, rehearse for something that, as it turned out, never happened. Kenneally was doing his duty at an 'emplacement', whether behind sandbags or dug into the earth, or both. The drawback with static defences was that they cramped the defenders and led to 'a passive spirit', according to an August 1940 Home Guard training instruction. Sooner rather than later, the British would need aggressive soldiers to go over to the attack, to throw the invaders back into the sea. A newspaper columnist quoted an anonymous friend who was on leave from the BEF after returning to England. He cycled to his family in the west of England. Guarding a small bridge in the Exe Valley were a corporal and two men with fixed bayonets. 'When I produced my pay book I said they had a good job. After Flanders it seemed a lovely way of spending a war. The corporal said I was wrong, it was an awful bore.' Guard duty did not only make a soldier go stale, it was a waste of what should have been a front line soldier.

For one of the many home defence handbook writers, Alfred Kerr, responsibility rested at the very lowest level, with the leader of a section of perhaps eight or ten men. Mostly, a section would work as an independent unit.

… it behoves the leader to act with initiative and resource. To obtain the best co-operation from his men he must get to know each one of his personnel and by the force of his own personality inspire confidence and that loyalty and discipline so essential for successful working under conditions of extreme hardship and danger.

Men should have confidence in themselves, and a team spirit, Kerr urged. The leader had to have confidence in himself; give a hearing to complaints; and enforce discipline on the march.

Interestingly, even regular Army commanders, who it might be thought would stick to tradition, were aware from the start of the need for Home Guards to show initiative – if only because no-one else was around to help. An undated document from a Colonel Fortescue of Southern Command is important because

Fig. 39

it is one of few – or at least few surviving – to set down, in the very earliest days of the preparations against invasion, what anyone had in mind after Eden's appeal over the radio. Fortescue was writing presumably in May 1940 because he used the term, 'volunteer defence force' (VDF), which soon disappeared in favour of LDV, then Home Guard. Fortescue began conventionally. Local commanders 'in consultation with lords lieuten-

JAMES HIPKISS

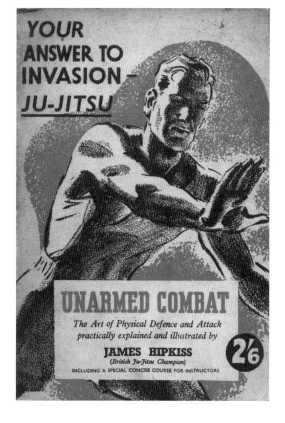

Fig. 52
(a) Bring your *left* foot *back* as you turn.

Fig. 53
(b) Lean well forward bending *right* knee deeply. 'Chop' *left* leg sharply.

Fig. 54
Turn half away and kick as you guard.

Fig. 55
Step well in and jab downward fiercely. Follow up with "leg lift and back heel" (47).

Fig. 57
(b) Pivot on *left* knee and throw all your weight against his thigh.

Fig. 58
Keep your back *flat*. Bend forward from your hips

Fig 59
Scoop *diagonally* forwards. Perform whole movement without the slightest hesitation

Drawings from *Unarmed Combat*, first issued in February 1941, by British ju-jitsu champion James Hipkiss (pictured far left). Hipkiss showed readers how to use their arms, legs and balanced body to outwit and knock out armed (and unarmed) Germans.

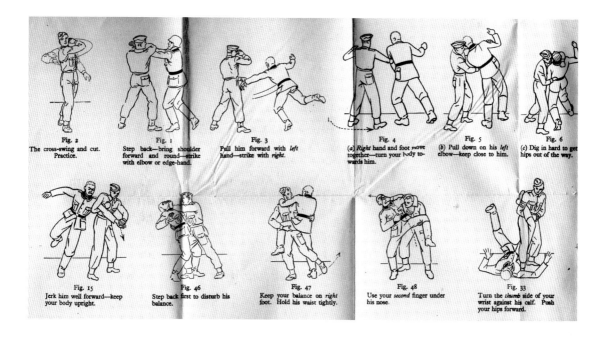

Fig. 2
The cross-swing and cut. Practice.

Fig. 1
Step back—bring shoulder forward and round—strike with elbow or edge-hand.

Fig. 3
Pull him forward with *left* hand—strike with *right*.

Fig. 4
(a) *Right* hand and foot move together—turn your body towards him.

Fig. 5
(b) Pull down on his *left* elbow—keep close to him.

Fig. 6
(c) Dig in hard to get hips out of the way.

Fig. 15
Jerk him well forward—keep your body upright.

Fig. 46
Step back first to disturb his balance.

Fig. 47
Keep your balance on *right* foot. Hold his waist tightly.

Fig. 48
Use your *second* finger under his nose.

Fig. 33
Turn the *thumb* side of your wrist against his calf. Push your hips forward.

ant', he explained, would select sub-area (that is, battalion) commanders. They would select company and platoon commanders, bearing 'local interests' in mind such as ex-servicemen's bodies – the British Legion, White Ensign Club, and Old Contemptibles. So far, it might look as though the Colonel was sticking to what he knew – tradition. But when he came to methods, Fortescue wrote: 'The VDF will come into force to deal with the enemy arriving by whatever means. The essence of their action is rapidity. It will be the responsibility of the commander of the local VDF unit to take action on his own initiative.'

For a senior Army officer to leave fighting – and the decision how to fight – to a volunteer was remarkable, even if it was only because the country was desperate.

LEADERS AND DISCIPLINE

The lack of leadership from the Army meant that the volunteers were required, amongst themselves or with help, to identify – and quickly – the right men to tell the rest what to do. Teachers and students could only spare so much time to improve their military skills; they had their full-time work. Besides guarding, recalled Bill Mycock, a Home Guard at Monyash, a farming village near Buxton, men were milking, morning and night: 'It was killing.' Nor could you assume that all the men were bright enough to be taught.

> I bought my own [books]. I used to go one night a week to the Drill Hall, Buxton, the officers would take not only me but the whole squad as well and give them some tuition. It was like talking to a brick wall, because they weren't educated.

The Monyash men were patrolling from Flagg Moor racecourse – they had the jockeys' quarters – to the Bull I' th' Thorn pub, still on the main road to Buxton. 'You knew people, you knew how much you could depend on them. I hate to say it because some of them have passed on but they didn't know their left from their right.'

That said, even among common labourers were some men with military experience who could tell other men what to do. Such leaders in their villages or workplaces might not be the obvious ones in peacetime society. In south Lincolnshire, one Home Guard company commander asked Walter Bannister, a farm worker, to be company sergeant major. Bannister, born in 1893, ran away from home at thirteen to enlist as a boy soldier. He served 21 years as a regular soldier: in India, in Mesopotamia during the First World War, then Baku. He returned to his village of Donington near Spalding. Bannister told his local newspaper in 1969 about his 1940: 'I could be working in the fields all day taking orders, but once on duty they knew what I was.'

One of many signs of a world turned upside down was such a reversal of rank. Fred Barratt said on this point:

> The call went out, and everybody volunteered. It was war, and we were really keyed up for this. A man possibly served in the First World War as a young man, would be given a commission, maybe like I was, second lieutenant, and they had got men in the unit who just volunteered and they [the First World War veterans] were professional people. But I think the spirit of it was, you were civilian volunteers and everybody was so prepared to work together, really and truly. That was the big thing, you couldn't have the discipline you could have in the Army because you were a civilian really, basically. We never had a chance to see how things would have worked. If he [Hitler] had invaded, it would immediately have become a unit and mixing with the Army and full time military. And it worked, the whole thing worked. It's surprising, really, how it did …

Major Eadie, his company commander, 'was well known and very much well liked', but as a painter and decorator Eadie was not of a higher social rank than some platoon commanders beneath him. Mr Hodgson, Fred's platoon commander and works manager, was jealous of Eadie, Fred recalled.

Some of the comedy of the BBC's *Dad's Army* about a Home Guard platoon arose from this tension between social class and military rank. On the difference between his factory work and the Home Guard, Fred Barratt said: 'At your work you were paid. Your works manager gave the orders, you accepted it, well, he was the boss.' As second in command to Mr Hodgson, Fred felt in 'a difficult position, because it was completely voluntary, you could say the rest of the unit took orders from me, but on a voluntary basis.'

Did one (the workplace) affect the other (the Home Guard)? Fred Barratt pulled up one man once, who called him Fred. At Fred's factory, his original rank was sergeant, below Mr Hodgson, the works manager and commander, and above the men. Home Guard rank often mirrored workplace rank. Frictions could arise in the workplace because the demands of military commanders were of a different sort to a civilian's at work. The LDV and then Home Guard was voluntary, whereas in the Army men were paid to do as they were told. Fred recalled that he used to say: 'You address me by rank, not the man.'

> … I know it was a bit of a try on, because he worked under me, he worked on a centre lathe. Well, he was very sloppy and I pulled him up and I said to him, 'Do the job properly… next time, just remember you salute and you say sir' … But we did impress upon them if we have to mobilise for invasion, for heaven's sake get it into your heads you are in the Army and you go straight under military discipline.

THE AIR FORCE – BOMBING THEIR OWN PEOPLE?

The uncomfortable truth was that failure in France had been very swift and compared badly with how the previous generation had done in the First World War. France had fallen at least partly because of Allied shortcomings in the air, whether because the Germans had more or better aeroplanes, or the French and British did not use their own as well as the Germans used theirs.

According to an official summary of home defence forces dated 13 June, the Air Force was the most forward-fighting part: 'Plan is reconnaissance of Continental ports to detect signs of concentration of expedition dusk and dawn, reconnaissance of continental and English coast, striking forces at seaborne expeditions, attacks on attempted landings, fighter interception of air raiders.'

The 'interception of air raiders' became the Battle of Britain, by far the most famous event of 1940 (for Britain). Yet the Air Force had much to think about in case of invasion, even while France was in the fight. Commander in Chief of Bomber Command, Charles Portal, wrote to the Air Ministry on 26 May that his Blenheim squadrons were anxious to do anything to help the Army and would gladly face the heaviest losses if it was worthwhile. 'After two weeks' experience however I am convinced that it is little short of folly to use these squadrons in the way in which I am most often asked to use them, namely to retrieve a situation on the ground that was already desperately serious at the time when the appeal was made.' Rarely would the Air Force be given a named target, such as a bridge. Instead, bomber crews were expected to look for their own. In Portal's opinion, these operations were 'little short of gestures'. Steadily they drained crews at the rate of one or two squadrons a week. 'It is the height of unwisdom to throw the Blenheims away in an attempt to do the work of artillery.' Portal intended to conserve the Blenheim force.

The Cabinet vetoed this policy on 7 June for political reasons: medium bombers had to make a maximum effort from the UK to co-ordinate with the French. France soon fell anyway. All this goes to show what was in the back of the Air Force commanders' minds, as they faced an invasion. If valuable bombers and their crews had to be lost, they were best lost attacking the most worthwhile targets. The unanswered question for the Air Force remained how, or indeed whether, to support soldiers on the ground.

A Home Forces paper dated 15 August admitted 'Employment of our bombers was largely influenced by consideration of the desperate needs of our allies, a handicap from which we are now free.' The home defence command considered purely in military terms how the Air Force ought to fight an invader, leaving aside the fact that British civilians might be underneath the bombs.

Discussing Blenheim (that is, medium bomber) support of the Army, the paper likened bombers to long range artillery, except bombers did not have the accuracy of artillery, nor the same intensity. Nor could bombers tell friend from foe as easily.

A Bristol Blenheim Mark IV, 'BL-R', of 40 Squadron RAF, 2 Group, based at Wyton, Huntingdonshire, photographed while on a daylight reconnaissance sortie to Abbeville during the Battle of France. Once France was lost, Royal Air Force commanders debated how to use such bombers over Britain.

The Germans were skilled at intense anti-aircraft fire, forcing bombers to fly above 6,000 feet, which would make it difficult to pick out small targets. In other words, bombers were 'most effective against targets that can easily be defined and found … against small or partly concealed targets bombing attack may have disappointing results.' The paper claimed that bridges were too narrow, and armoured columns usually too spread out, to be damaged by bombing.

Summing up, Home Forces reckoned that close support by Blenheims was unlikely to turn the balance for ground defences. Instead, ships unloading stores, and dumps, would 'repay sustained attacks' by Blenheims. The paper concluded that best use of Blenheims would be to attack ships and disembarking troops, landing points and defiles where roads were congested.

So much for what the Air Force would try to bomb, after an invasion. Who would tell them to bomb what? In an exchange of letters and meetings in August, Bomber Command held on to control of bombers in an invasion. General Brooke admitted privately that a problem following an invasion would be how to decide between 'competing claims'. He did not add on paper that Churchill, someone who loved to stick his nose into military matters, might try to have a say, and botch it.

In September GHQ Home Forces called on Army commands to practise wireless or other emergency communications between army headquarters and bomber stations. The point was that 'central control may disappear'; if so, Air

Prime Minister Winston Churchill with a Tommy gun, on a tour of coastal defences near Hartlepool, 31 July 1940.

Above left: The Houses of Parliament. As a veteran of the Battle of Omdurman and the trenches in the First World War, Churchill could not resist poking his nose into the defences of central government buildings around Whitehall.

Above right: Wellington Arch and Piccadilly. The parks of central London, it was feared, could be parachutist or glider landing grounds.

Force commanders had to ask for targets from their nearest army commander, or do their own air reconnaissance. As a sign of how desperate the defence could become, operational training unit (OTU) aircraft – and presumably their half-trained crews – would replace 'wastage' in front line units. GHQ proposed to improvise a striking force of Lysanders, small reconnaissance aeroplanes that were never meant to be bombers.

Meanwhile the Battle of Britain raged. Fighter squadrons by day sought to beat the German Luftwaffe over the south and east of England. Bomber squadrons by night tried to hit continental ports where the Germans were collecting shipping. One of the little-appreciated facts of 1940 is that more men died in Bomber Command than Fighter Command during the Battle of Britain, if only because a bomber had several crewmen. Only much later did doubts arise as to how much difference the bombers made. In January 1942, Slessor wrote from RAF 5 Group to Air Vice Marshal H.H. Bottomley, then Deputy Chief of Air Staff. Slessor was looking for evidence about how much damage the RAF bombing of invasion ports in the autumn of 1940 did to German preparations. He had gone into results of later enemy bombing of Southampton and Liverpool, and was 'rather astonished at the small extent to which capacity of Liverpool as a military embarkation port was reduced [by] serious blitzes' in May 1941. Work did come to a standstill, but only because of the 'indisciplined civilian dockers' who would not turn up. The British could not count on that at French invasion ports. That remark suggests the British still had a lingering fear of invasion. It did not seem to occur to Slessor or Bottomley, or anyone else in a blue uniform, that all their bombing of Germany might not do much good either.

GAS

It was one thing for the Royal Air Force to bomb its own bridges and ports, another to drop poison gas, likely to spread over a wider area. Yet the RAF did look into the practical aspects. An air vice marshal at GHQ Home Forces asked on 5 August if Lysander, Battle and Blenheim squadrons had gas stocks, what were the reserves, and whether gas spray containers would be refilled at the aerodrome or the gas-making factory. And how long would it take for squadrons to change from bombs to gas, if use of gas was authorised after an invasion? Appreciating that some leakage was unavoidable, he advised that gas attack aircraft should be down-wind of an aerodrome.

The RAF confirmed that mustard gas spray was at five Lysander squadrons – Grangemouth, Linton on Ouse, Hatfield, West Malling, and Old Sarum; enough

Australian soldiers in gas masks and a Vickers heavy machine gun in August 1940. Might the British have dropped poison gas from the air in an effort to drive invaders into the sea?

for two squadron sorties. Besides, there was a reserve stock. The Air Force returned containers empty to the factory, and they came back in a week to squadron, depending on transport. There were enough gas bombs for one or two squadron sorties and about 7,000 gas bombs in reserve.

The RAF would drop a low spray against troops in the open, and gas bombs 'where contamination of installations and focal points is required', depending on the tactical situation. It was not 'present policy' to gas initial enemy landings. The Air Force was sure that leakage was slight and could be ignored. A switch in armament to gas would take 24 hours. If the enemy went inland, the Air Force could not say if it would have permission to drop gas. There was the civil population 'to consider'. As minutes of a meeting at the Air Ministry on 27 June said, the Cabinet would have to sanction use of gas 'in view of our international undertaking not to use gas unless it is first used against us'.

Later in August, the RAF confirmed that a dozen Lysanders could be switched to gas in six hours, and the CiC Home Forces asked regional commands to train in gas spraying with the Air Force. But there was not enough training liquid for all commands to train at once.

Another meeting at the Air Ministry, on Saturday 14 September, reviewed RAF chemical warfare. Those attending wondered whether a Ministry of Supply officer with chemical experience might buy phosgene bombs in the US, but they spoke of 'political objections', presumably from the Americans, to the export. Besides, the Admiralty 'might have views on their ships in convoy being loaded with phosgene bombs'. As the meeting noted, phosgene was lethal but not persistent; all Britain's gas bombs were mustard, which was persistent but not lethal.

This RAF chemical warfare committee, chaired by Air Vice Marshal Douglas, admitted it (still) did not know the political position on operational use of gas. It did know that wearing a gas respirator restricted vision and 'causes nervousness among troops who know it may be lurking around the next corner'.

Any cover such as trees reduced casualties from spray. Low attacks were most effective but brought danger from anti-aircraft guns. Suggested was high spray, for 'nuisance value', especially at night. The meeting concluded that 'gas will never stop a determined enemy; fire [bullets and shells] alone will do this … gas in spite of its limitations is a potent weapon. It harasses and tends to demoralise an opponent and slows up his operations and movements.' The meeting proposed the best use of gas bombs was against docks, and spray was best in the open. Low spray should be used in 'forward areas', that is, nearer battlefields, and high spray only in the rear, because of 'danger to our troops'. Chemical warfare training should be in the syllabus at bomber OTU (training) squadrons. In November 1940, the Air Force ordered 846 containers of 500lb mustard gas bombs for use by Blenheim and Wellington squadrons.

TO THE LAST MAN?

The official summary of home defence forces dated 13 June quoted above was as follows:

> Outline of plan is material obstruction and land mining of likely landing beaches with defensive positions in most vulnerable areas which will be held at all costs; mobile columns available to move quickly to threatened areas; one division in general reserve.

The phrase 'at all costs' kept cropping up all summer. It came from the very top. 'We will never surrender,' said Churchill. If you did not surrender, he implied, you won, or fought to the death. Not everyone spelt it out so starkly, 'to the death', yet this was official policy that trickled down to the defenders. Aldridge Home Guard battalion in Staffordshire received its 'operational orders number one' by telephone on 5 July. 'Reliable reports state that attack on this country is imminent …. Companies will pin down, defeat and destroy any enemy who may land …. There must not and will not be any question of retirement.'

If the enemy had reached that area in any force, they could have seized the high ground overlooking Birmingham and so threatened most north-south and east-west communications. England would have been as good as lost; the defenders would not have had many defensible places to retire to.

Why then the insistent tone, implying that if you did not destroy the enemy, it would be you who was destroyed? The volunteers had to hold, to give time for the regular army to arrive. In later recollections, the veterans agreed; it would have been a fight to the death – their deaths, probably. Reginald Titt, the Salisbury LDV man who worked at Porton Down, was in charge of moveable tank obstacles, as used to close important roads at the last minute. 'In our case the obstacles

Men of 7th Battalion, the Green Howards on guard duty inside a blockhouse at Sandbanks, near Poole in Dorset. Such men on the very front line were expected to stay and fight until relieved – or dead. (War Office official photograph, 31 July 1940)

were made of angled pieces of railway line or heavy steel girders which took two or three men to move. With practice we could block the Wilton Road at the junction with Highbury Avenue in about half a minute.' His unit's job was then to stop the enemy moving the blocks.

> We had little prospect of holding the attackers off for long, but if they could be delayed significantly at every block, the cumulative effect of the delays was expected to allow mobile Army units to get to the scene. In effect we were trained and equipped to fight and almost certainly lose a nasty little battle that might last half an hour.

Teenage Buxton Home Guard man Rob Butler said that 'last man, last round' was no secret. 'In the early days it was last scythe, last sword, it was as bad as that. In the first days we didn't have any arms at all, except for the odd shotgun, we didn't even have any uniform for quite a while.' In Staffordshire Fred Barratt, asked about orders to fight to the last round, last man, answered: 'I think it was an accepted fact.'

Defenders would have fought grimly partly out of fear of what the Nazis would do to them – and everyone else. Commanders such as Lieutenant-General G.C. Williams, Commander in Chief Eastern Command, stressed this in a September 1940 message calling on Home Guards to make every effort: '… remember that every successful defence of a village, every offensive act carried out by day or night will reduce the area temporarily occupied by the enemy and the numbers of old people and women and children who will have to suffer the indignities or worse of such occupation.'

Nor was the situation hidden from the public. A Press Association reporter in mid-July, spreading it thick, wrote in a widely-printed article: 'Should an invading German force come out of the morning North Sea mist and cutting through the protective screen of the British Navy and the RAF succeed in making landings here, they will come face to face with regiments of an army ordered to fight to the last man.' He quoted a major 'in a famous Scottish unit which saw service in France': 'There is no question of our retiring to a second line defence.'

Such orders came from the very top. At a meeting on 29 June 1940, General Sir Edmund Ironside, the then Commander in Chief Home Forces, reported to the highest Air Force and Navy chiefs and Generals Sir John Dill and 'Pug' Ismay of the War Cabinet Office. Ironside spoke of 'very few troops in depth as local reserves' behind the beach defences. 'It had however been made quite clear in the operational instructions issued by GHQ Home Forces that there was to be no withdrawal from the beach defences and that the troops in them were to fight it out where they stood.' In other words, victory or death.

What is not appreciated is that fighting to the end and not surrendering, though despised as fanatical when the Japanese did it in 1945, was what British

South Staffordshire Home Guards at Barr Beacon.

soldiers were supposed to do anyway. As the War Office Infantry Training manual 1937 for infantry battalions put it,

> All ranks should understand that the troops allotted to the defence of a post or locality are responsible for holding it at all costs and for inflicting the greatest possible loss upon the enemy. All ranks should realise that it is a disgrace to lay down their arms in the field. If ammunition is exhausted recourse should be had to a final effort with the bayonet.

From the start of invasion defence, though, as Churchill (and others in the know) were aware, some defenders would not fight to the last – or rather they would, but in hiding.

GUERRILLAS

Some time in the middle of 1940, a man of the village of Quarr near Ryde on the Isle of Wight, S.A. Watson, took a telephone call from Captain R.G.B. Spicer, the island's Chief Constable. He asked Watson to come to his office at Fairlee, Newport, the island's main town.

'I was shown in to Captain Spicer who had with him a man in civilian clothes,' Watson recalled years later. 'Captain Spicer asked me what I proposed to do if the island were occupied by German forces. I replied that I should remain in the island in the capacity of executive officer of the Isle of Wight war agricultural executive committee.' Spicer then asked Watson to meet a man in a car in the yard. 'I naturally asked Captain Spicer who this man was and he replied that he, Captain Spicer, would vouch for his identity and purpose. I was somewhat interested in this cloak and dagger business ...' Safe from eavesdroppers the man, a Major Saunders, said he had been sent by the War Office to interview Watson.

The major gave his life history, which 'astonished' Watson, though tantalisingly he did not say why.

> He told me that the British Government through their agents in the German War Office were in the possession of all the alternative plans for the invasion of this country. But what they did not know was which plan the Germans would put into operation and that would only be known when the event took place. So far as our part of the country was concerned a plan was to seize the Isle of Wight and thereby dominate and control Portsmouth naval dockyard and the port of Southampton. The plan he submitted to me was that I should organise a set of people throughout the island who lived no more than three miles apart but the set-up should cover the whole island. These men should be known only to me and not to one another. It was vital to the plan that one should have a boat and to know the Solent so that messages could be passed across the water. Major Saunders would train me in the act of simple sabotage such as gelignite explosive and petrol bombs and in turn I would instruct the others. I agreed to co-operate.

First, Watson sounded out Leonard P. New Jr. of Messrs W.B. Mew Langton, the Newport brewers. Watson and Mew had been at school together. Mew was a yachting man with a motor cruiser. Watson recruited several others, including Tom Cowley of Stenbury Manor, Whitwell. All Watson's recruits met at Stenbury Manor. Each agreed to recruit four or five in their locality. In some secluded spot in their patch would be built an underground chamber: '... to be of sufficient size that the party could live in it and it could store equipment and ammunition and such like'. For their own band Mew and Watson recruited three more men, including a café licensee, based in a dugout in a wood. They enlisted as members of the Home Guard.

Years later Watson typed his story – note, in passing, once again the crucial role of police as gate-keepers – now in the Isle of Wight record office. While it was unusual for a resistance organiser to put his story on record, it is stretching the truth to call these men a 'secret army', as some historians have. In his war memoir, Churchill printed an August 1940 memo to Eden, asking about progress of 'new guerrilla formations of the Home Guard known as auxiliary units'.

These units were indeed within the 'general body of Home Guard' as a document dated 26 July 1940 said. Their role was 'to act offensively on the flanks and

Left: The front cover of the best-selling 1940 *New Ways of War* by Tom Wintringham. As the title suggested, it stressed the need to learn from guerrillas and left-wing fighters of the 1936–9 civil war in Spain. The Oxford *Dictionary of National Biography* described the remarkable Wintringham – imprisoned for sedition in the 1920s and founder of the *Daily Worker* – as a 'uniquely English revolutionary'.

Below: Home Guard tactics were hard to agree on. Should the defenders seek to take on any invaders even if better trained and equipped, or seek to blend in – three riflemen are in this picture – and strike at small enemy bands?

in the rear of any German troops who may obtain a temporary foothold in this country', and to gather intelligence. 'Their task is to harry and embarrass the enemy by all means in their power from the first day he lands; their particular targets being tanks and lorries in laager, ammunition dumps, hqs, small straggling parties and posts etc.'

They would mainly work by night. These were local men who knew their countryside intimately: farmers, game keepers and hunt servants. These occupations echo what happened on the Isle of Wight where those originally selected, mostly well-off men, chose from the lower classes too. Those chosen would occupy prepared hideouts 'in heath or woodlands'; this too supported the Isle of Wight organiser's story.

How many 'auxiliaries' were there? By 26 July 1940, one IO (intelligence officer) covered Essex and Suffolk, one covered Lincolnshire and one covered north-east Scotland and the west Highlands. Three officers across Hampshire-Wiltshire-Dorset-Somerset-Devon-Cornwall worked for ten days and enrolled 200 men. In Eastern Command, three IOs had been at work for three weeks, and in Norfolk an IO was about to start; 250 men enrolled in all. Northern Command had 100 men enrolled. One IO was about to go to South Wales. The document reported no difficulty in finding men. Lower priority areas such as North Wales and the Midlands had not been 'opened up'. So far the IOs were single-handed, but would need regular troops under them for training the auxiliaries.

In a summer when organisers feared time was short, it helped that some guerrilla equipment as suggested by 'Yank' Levy, Tom Wintringham's teacher on the subject, was readily available. You could smear strips of burnt cork across the face as black camouflage. Other things took time and effort, such as hideouts. Levy advised that like the Irish Republican Army on the run, once a hide-out was built and memorised, guerrillas should not go back to it, because you never knew who might observe you.

Some, such as the young, relished it all. Cecil Thronalley, of Swineshead in Lincolnshire, a teenage auxiliary, recalled 'You were trained to fight with a knife so you wouldn't make any noise.'

All the secrecy could lead to misunderstandings. Rob Marshall, a child in Shanklin on the Isle of Wight, was amongst boys who found a cave containing food, a chemical toilet, rifles, hand grenades and boxes of explosives. The boys took it to be a spy's hide-out, and told the police. The Army blew the hole up. Dick Wheway, a local Home Guard officer, ordered the boys to keep it secret. After the war Rob Marshall asked Wheway to explain. The boys had found a 'behind the lines' hideaway: 'As we had discovered it shortly after it had been stocked I cannot think its camouflage would have been too effective.'

Despite the necessary secrecy, auxiliary units did have some paperwork. One group, presumably by mistake, let theirs pass to Somerset record office in Taunton. According to the training, a scout patrol was to have at most a leader and four others. They were to carry a revolver, more suited to close-up fighting than a heavier rifle, a Mills bomb, truncheon or fighting knife, and field dressing: 'Each man should be a complete demolition unit in himself.' For quietness the patrollers were to wear gym shoes, except in the wet; then footwear would be a rubber agricultural ankle boot.

> Your task is either to destroy by incendiarism, demolition or ambush, enemy stores, aeroplanes and vehicles, or to overpower isolated sentries, stragglers, hq DRs [headquarters despatch riders]. You must therefore lie low if encountered by an enemy patrol and never accept battle unless the odds are overwhelmingly in your favour. Whilst en route to your task do not return the enemy's fire.

Similarly if ambushing convoys, the group should avoid a 'free fight' and destroy lorries with stores rather than their escorts, and always with a getaway route. For demolitions, the auxiliaries should use a time pencil: 'Remember we want to be back in bed before the explosion occurs.' Headquarters advised men to never leave a wounded comrade, and to try to take him to a friend's house rather than their base.

While a region might only have a few hundred such guerrillas, each patrol of five officially had a 2.5-mile radius. Many, so it was claimed, were confident of covering four times the area, in other words operating as far as five miles from base. Between them, auxiliaries could range over most parts. By day, an observer might make a traffic census of a main road, seeking targets for the night. The auxiliary by day ought to wear, rather than a balaclava and black face, a face of light strawberry bed netting, decorated with green and brown cloth or with leaves or grass. Nothing should be cumbersome, because the observer had to move fast 'with eyes in the back of his head'. He ought to have a place to hide if enemy came near, to go to ground, apart from the unit's OB [operational base]. An observer's OB would not necessarily be a hole in the ground (as discovered on the Isle of Wight); it could be a cellar in a broken down building or a cluster of thick bushes. Essential were 'good camouflage, weather-proofing and ease of access'.

Headquarters admitted that the thrill of the secret fight could fade through hardship and boredom. Men should harden their bodies to exposure, fatigue, thirst, hunger and other discomforts – likened to hardening a greenhouse plant before putting it in the garden. Training discussed how heat was produced in the body, lost, and retained. When sleeping out on cold nights, men should lie with their head in the sleeping bag, or breathe through a scarf wrapped loosely about the face.

Mental dullness was 'inevitable', the trainers admitted. They suggested 'mental gymnastics' such as Pelmanism ('the science and art of self-realization'). In that vein headquarters warned auxiliaries to 'beware of pessimism and despondency, which are the natural outcome of failure and casualties.' A 'typical' 24-hour winter's day in the field was Spartan – lights out at 7am, reveille at 2.30pm, outside at 8.30pm for 15 minutes to acclimatise to the dark, then march off on patrol.

Trainers told the guerrillas how to make ambushes. If against motorcycle riders, wire stretched across the road at body height would 'probably' decapitate the rider. If attacking an infantry patrol in a lorry, the auxiliaries should remain farther away and rely on heavy automatic fire during the confusion. Once any organised defence began, they should retire. To merely 'annoy' the enemy on a road, they should fell a tree, or set a booby trap.

What the trainers could not offer, if the invasion came, was any news about the guerrillas' families, or much idea about what good the guerrillas were doing, or how many days they had to live.

THEORY AND REALITY – STOP LINES AND FIELDS

Guerrillas in the English countryside would – as they did later in Yugoslavia and Russia – annoy the invaders and then, when the war began to turn against the invading forces, cause genuine strategical damage. But to beat an invader, while yet taking into account how weak and unprepared the defence was, was a matter of strategy for the higher commanders. Their plan optimistically cast the defenders as sheepdogs and the invaders the penned sheep – if the enemy would stay in the pens.

An early word on strategy came from Southern Command, dated 22 June. It admitted some areas had no field force formations to round up 'hostiles'. The command spoke wishfully of eventual lines of stops organised into 'a proper defensive position based on an anti-tank obstacle with wire with fields of fire from a concrete pillbox system distributed in depth covering that obstacle … This however is a state of affairs which will not arise in the immediate future.' Their immediate aim was 'to divide England into several small fields surrounded by hedges of anti-tank obstacles' and use natural ground where possible. If enemy tanks or paratroops broke into an 'enclosure', the Command proposed 'to close the gates by blocking the crossings over the obstacles and to let in the dogs in the shape of armoured formations or other troops to round up the cattle'. The document listed the 'fields' in its region: a) the River Perrett through Bridgewater to the Taunton railway to Ilminster and the River Axe to Chard, Axminster and Seaton; b) the River Frome, from Bradford on Avon to Frome, then the Wylye valley to Salisbury and the River Avon to Ringwood and Christchurch; and c) the railway from Salisbury to Romsey along the Test to Stockbridge, then along the railway to Whitchurch and to Basingstoke to another 'GHQ' stop line.

To turn the shepherding metaphors and lines on the map into a real defence began with surveying, towards the end of June. Western Command for example, covering the far north-west of England and Wales, was to build 'GHQ reserve'

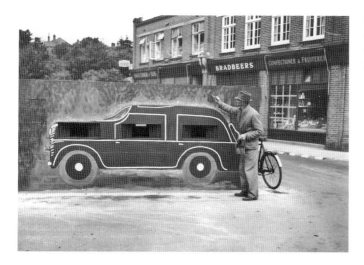

Pillbox camouflaged as a car in Felixstowe. (War Office official photograph, August 1940)

A view north over the Dove Valley in southern Derbyshire including a pillbox on the valley side, sited in case of attack from the north.

positions, from Rugby to Kidderminster and Leamington to the north of Banbury, to meet Southern Command. The work fell to some quite junior Royal Engineers – in this case, to Alan West who had recently finished a six-month officer's course at Aldershot by doing the conga at a sappers' ball.

> Each morning I was to rendezvous with Lieutenant Colonel Walker of the North Lancs Regiment. Starting at Leamington we marched day after day along the railway line to Rugby. Being allergic to pollens, I sneezed my head off amid the long grass and flowers on the embankments and cuttings. We stopped at every bridge, culvert or tactical strongpoint, discussed how the enemy would come and agreed the location of strong points and demolitions necessary.
>
> Despite the urgency of our task Colonel Walker was not going to allow us to drop with exhaustion. He had an old saloon car, driven by Mrs Walker, a seasoned army wife with a little daughter of about ten. She would drive us to our starting point each morning and then, synchronising watches in true Army style, meet us at an agreed map reference for midday lunch of sandwiches and other goodies from a hamper she had prepared.
>
> As the Colonel and I appeared over the horizon she would stop knitting and produce the picnic. For an hour peace would reign amid the buzzing of the bees and the perfume of the flowers in little Miss Walker's garlands. Halcyon days!
>
> Nearing Rugby we discovered the Dun Cow at Dunchurch to be a convenient headquarters for lunch, Perhaps Mrs Walker had become tired of making sandwiches. Beyond Rugby we struck north, using the A5 road as the defence line until we reached Tamworth. There, under an archway leading to the courtyard of this ancient hostelry, a much faded sign beside a bell pull said 'Ring for Ostler'! Here ended our section of the Birmingham Defence Line reconnaissance.

Meanwhile in Northern Ireland, according to *Life's Rich Pageant*, broadcaster Arthur Marshall's autobiography, Army officers in civilian clothes were going into southern Ireland in civilian clothes, 'feeling rather daredevil', to measure roads and bridges, in case the British had to drive into Eire to throw out Germans.

Another early paper dated 23 June admitted 'rather uncontrolled beginnings' concerning road blocks. The policy had 'crystallised' – into the hope that the enemy, not knowing the country well, would 'probably' fight shy of minor roads, especially 'thick country'. Hence blocks around ports, probable landing beaches and landing grounds, and, on maps at least, the 'anti-tank stop lines'. Main roads had to stay free of blocks so the defenders could speed to the invader. By 12 July Auchinleck, as head of Southern Command, was stressing that his whole policy for defence was based on mobility. That meant moveable (lighter) blocks only on the main roads, such as 'derelict lorries filled with cement, steam rollers, traction engines, threshing machines etc.' Presumably the invaders would want to use the main roads, too? As the military admitted, such a block could 'never permanently block a road against serious attempts to pass by heavy tracked vehicles'. But, it would 'undoubtedly stop or seriously delay light reconnaissance vehicles including light tanks'.

In any case, the stop lines needed far more men and dug defences than would ever be available. On 4 July, for instance, Salisbury Plain area reported to Southern Command that except at mills, the River Wylye was 'in no sense a tank obstacle', as it was supposed to be; the river was fordable almost everywhere. The report totted up the scores of blocks and pillboxes, and the thousands of mines required to defend the line, and concluded that

> The line affords no depth whatsoever. The defence is barely linear and if a determined attack were made upon it by enemy tanks they would undoubtedly penetrate somewhere and create a gap which would render the remainder of the line useless.

Here Southern Command gave up a line in this part of Wiltshire and instead defended with a 'mobile striking force' fourteen places – villages such as Maiden Bradley and Codford St Mary; Witton with its dozen road and railway bridges; and towns too large to leave, such as Warminster and Salisbury.

It was the same around the country. The generals with their high ideas and drawings on maps were fooling themselves. As a Warwickshire Home Guard historian recalled, the original plan was to meet the enemy at the outskirts of every hamlet. Home Guards in 'penny packets' at each village and road junction 'would be annihilated piecemeal'. For instance, the company around Brinklow had to cover the canal as a 'stop-line'.

> As it was perfectly obvious that anything less than a brigade could not hope to man the indicated stretch of canal throughout its length of some two miles the plan of defence was simplified to that of holding the main road bridges. The fact that there were several subsidiary bridges carrying farm tracks and the like over this 'defended' stretch of water was as obvious to higher authority as it would have been to the enemy … But the Home Guard had been reared on a diet of forlorn hopes and the tactical disabilities were accepted in a spirit of cheerful resignation to fate. A fairly early abandonment of the stop line defence was accepted without tears.

Role, training, weapons and tactics affected each other as much for guerrillas as for home defenders in general. Street fighting, and staying alive in the countryside by blending into the landscape during a bewildering invasion when the telephones and radios went dead, would demand more shadowy, small-scale, guerrilla warfare. This called for, as Yank Levy said, caution, invisibility and surprise. In other words, you needed the right attitude rather than the ordinary soldier's weapons – 'the really difficult thing is to get a man to use his head when hell is popping … a good guerrilla fighter must out-smart, out-think the other fellow.'

Geography mattered too, because – to hark back to Churchill's 'we shall fight them on the beaches' speech – landing grounds, fields, streets and hills offered different landscapes for the attacker and defender. It did not matter how smart a guerrilla fought if he did not have a place to hide. Guerrilla warfare, as Liddell Hart wrote later in the war, was most effective where populations were small, 'the area wide, and communications scanty'. That was not true for much of Britain, let alone the Continent-facing part, rural and urban, that would face any invader first.

CHAPTER 5

TOWN, COAST AND COUNTRY

Local patriotism is the rock upon which national unity is founded. It is the source from which national effort draws its strength.
A.H. Blake, Burton upon Trent borough director of education, preface to Charles Underhill's *History of Burton*, 1941

Time mattered in Britain in the summer of 1940; would the defences be ready before the Germans were ready to invade? Place mattered too; would the Germans invade – and they could land where they pleased, or not at all – where the defenders were weakest? Imagining invasion was not only done out of fear – it made military sense to think like the enemy, all the better to counter him. Thus at dinner at Chequers on 6 September, Churchill 'placed himself in the position of Hitler and attacked these isles while I defended them', Brooke wrote in his diary. As in a game of football, the German way in 1940 was to use speed and teamwork. They did not use any new weapons, merely a fresh combination of existing ones, in order to put armies where their enemy did not want them to be. An army like France's or Britain's, used to the 1914–18 pace of war and fighting in a line, fell aside like a dam breached by water. Men of Dumfriesshire and Shropshire taking to arms, scores or even hundreds of miles from any likely German landing grounds, were paying a compliment to the German successes of 1939 and 1940. Remarkably quickly, Britain appreciated what became known as *blitzkrieg* – lightning war. Lightning can strike anywhere. Briefly, spearheads – of tanks, aided by dive-bombers and other aircraft, and maybe parachutists – pierced the line and once in the rear could paralyse the whole and go anywhere. War had changed its pace, from the three or four miles an hour of the First World War, as fast as an infantryman could walk, to the 30 mph of tanks, artillery and infantrymen carried by lorries – and the 350 mph of the diving Stuka.

Above left: The main street in Lockerbie in southern Scotland. Dumfriesshire and other remote parts of the country were last in the queue for Home Guard equipment – which meant in 1940 they got little or nothing.

Above right: The Devil's Punch Bowl at Hindhead on the border of Hampshire and Surrey, on the main Portsmouth to London road, the A3. Once any south coast invaders got ashore and over the top of the wolds and downs, there was little geographically to hinder them.

The bleaker truth, as past successful invaders proved, such as Duke William of Normandy in 1066, was that once the invader was ashore and saw off the worst that the defenders could do, usually not far inland, England lacked a wide river or mountains to hide behind to hold off the enemy while guarding the heart of the kingdom. The wealds of Kent and Lincolnshire and the waterways of East Anglia might slow an invader, but once ashore, the going was fairly flat until the hills roughly north and west of a line from the Bristol Channel to the Wash – but a defence behind that line gave up London, and other ports where the invader could bring in all the troops and supplies needed. In that case, a rallied defence would be as hopeless as it was for the French in early June 1940, on the line of the River Somme, even though Paris and the bulk of the country was unconquered.

Whether the Germans landed in the nearest counties, Sussex and Kent, or took a less direct route into Hampshire and Dorset and struck for north of the Thames from Salisbury Plain, or whether they sought to capture London in a pincer from the south and east – as the largest English counter-invasion exercise assumed in October 1941 – there was no obvious line of defence once the invader was ashore. The obvious natural defence was offshore – the Channel. As the MP and journalist Beverley Baxter put it in June 1940: 'We have two defences that are worth a dozen Maginot lines. One is the English Channel; the other is the Irish Sea.' As the French were about to surrender as those words went to print, readers might have wondered at Baxter's choice of metaphor. Yet France's Maginot line had worked, in a way: it had so deterred the Germans that they attacked else-where, all too well.

Brooke took over from Ironside as CiC Home Forces on 20 July. Ironside left 'not a word concerning the defences or his policy of defence, etc, absolutely nothing!' Brooke fumed in his diary. The new man argued for what he termed an 'active counter offensive' rather than 'linear defence'. For all the tinkering, only natural when one commander takes over from another and gives different weight to parts of the job, England's land defence, based on geography, almost set up itself. London, the important high ground around it, airfields and ports and what General Brooke termed 'endless vulnerable points requiring guards', all had to be denied to the enemy.

In truth, not least to fit the LDV into the defence and because of the genuine need for the LDV to guard so many places, Brooke or any other commander had both linear and active policies. This was not quite the same 'either-or' as static or mobile. England did not have enough LDVs or any other bodies to make a static but unbroken line; it could only manage 'stop lines' and 'defended places', to hold the enemy for the mobile reserve to finish off. Or so the generals hoped.

EDEN'S UNDERSTANDABLE MISTAKE

Eden in his 14 May appeal had, in as many words, told large towns that they did not need extra guarding: 'This appeal is directed chiefly to those who live in small towns, villages and less densely inhabited suburban areas. I must warn you that for certain military reasons there will be some localities where the numbers required will be small and others where your services will not be required at all.'

Where cities did recruit volunteers in the first days, it was with an eye on the open spaces beyond, where parachutists might land. Lieutenant-Colonel F.A. Neill, commander of Sheffield Defence Volunteer Corps appealed for people in outlying districts 'to offer accommodation, even a barn, or a room for use of night patrols'. Neill appointed commanders in the south, east and west police divisions of Sheffield before central – implying that the centre of Sheffield was not so important.

Sheffield Town Hall Square and Burbage Moors. Although the city was plainly more important to an invader than moorland, the authorities in Sheffield originally left the city centre's defence until last, assuming paratroopers would land outside the built-up area.

The links at Carnoustie in Scotland. Once Germans used paratroopers with success on 10 May 1940, the British realised uneasily how many open spaces such as golf courses were potential landing grounds.

Eden had good reasons. Gliders and parachutists of course could not land safely in built-up areas. When in September 1944 the British paratroopers landed at Arnhem, they dropped not on the town, let alone at the objective, the Rhine bridge, but outside – hence the ensuing controversy; some argued that landing miles away had made the difference between success and tragic failure.

It is easy to forget how many English villages kept to themselves to themselves, hardly dealing with the world outside. Eden was seeking to remedy this with volunteer parachute-spotters. While leading men of a village might have professional work or leisure interests in the nearest town, the rank and file might seldom visit even the next village. In Staffordshire, a 'scattered' Home Guard company covered a mix of mining and farming villages from Great Wyrley to Shareshill and the Saredons. An officer in the Cannock Home Guard unit history admitted, 'Although we came from the same district we were on the whole strangers to one another.'

The literal and mental horizon of the average volunteer – apart perhaps from service abroad in 1914–18 – only went 'up the road'. Jim Trinder's father, in the Army Service Corps in the first war, was in the LDV in the village of Aldsworth, near Cirencester, 'not a very large place, there must have been 30 chaps that met on a Sunday. My dad had just an armband, and a stick. He used to go up the road, oh, a couple of times a week.' Nor did the townsman's horizon, or network of friends, family and workmates, necessarily stretch to the next town. George Lane, the watch and clock repairer in Kidderminster, made no mention in his diary of the 30 June 'Battle of Bewdley' in the next town, a couple of miles away. As on 16 July he was writing 'All comparatively quiet', it is hard to believe he would have ignored the 'battle' if someone had told him about it. Given such ignorance of close localities, you have to suspect that a German parachutist landing in Bewdley would have been at large for ages.

Town and country in 1940 often blurred. For instance, London County Council (LCC) mental hospitals were 'institutions in the main in extensive grounds which constitute potential landing places for parachutists and troop landing planes'. Guarding them was felt – by the council at least – to be crucial. Similarly, town and

A scene from the Cannock Home Guard history. A man armed with a truncheon (top), wearing civilian clothes except for the LDV armband says: 'Halt! Who goes there?' 'Company Commander', the approaching man answers. 'Stand fast mate while I pop and fetch a rifle outer th'ut.'

Colonel Maunders, Cannock battalion
commander.

city utilities such as waterworks
were in the country. The countryside around towns and cities was
often within walking distance.
That said, at first some town and
city commanders simply forgot
about some of their remoter units.
H.R. Oswald, as LCC's assistant
clerk based at County Hall, began
organising the LCC's volunteer
defenders. On 19 July Oswald
wrote to London LDV organisers,
admitting that having gone over
the 'rough skeleton organisation'
of his battalion, he had 'omitted
to mention' a unit of 110 men at
the council's emergency office at
Coopers Hill, Egham, on a hill
overlooking Windsor Castle.

COAST

In a minute about invasion dated 18 July, claiming that a 'surprise crossing' should
be impossible, Churchill reasoned that invasion of the south or east coast was
unlikely. He argued for bringing more divisions into support or reserve, to train
them for the offensive and as the coast became fortified, increasingly leaving
defence to other troops, such as the Home Guard. Churchill as a politician could
wish for things that the military might not be able to deliver.

The First Sea Lord tried to rein Churchill in by quoting a 1917 committee
on invasion that stated that although they could not guarantee a first invasion
convoy would not arrive, subsequent convoys would fail. Therefore British land
forces would have to deal with that first convoy. During the First World War, the
maximum of invading soldiers was put at 30,000. The 1940 maximum was set
at 50,000. The First Sea Lord ended: 'In calm, misty weather a large number of
vessels might start from the enemy shore' without being seen, and such a convoy
might reach the coast without the navy intercepting. The enemy's landfall would
be inaccurate, but 'there are so many places on our coast where landing is possible
that this might not be of vital importance.'

A suggested total of 97,000 might reach British shores without naval interception. Only 25,000 would land on the south coast (from French ports), compared
with 62,000 on the east coast (from German, Dutch and Belgian ports), and
10,000 in Scotland (from Norway).

To cover the hundreds of miles of beaches, the authorities turned to mines.
Lincolnshire was not the most continental-facing stretch of coast, but not the least
threatened. Its beaches and the sand dunes were basically out of bounds, Wainfleet
man K.G. Motley recalled, 'Many people lost their cats and dogs because they got
into the dunes and blew themselves up by triggering off mines.'

> Six-sided pill-boxes were dotted around. We [in Wainfleet] had one at the junc-
> tion of the High Street and St John's Street, where it commanded the level
> crossing over the railway just at the station; at points like that, where there was
> a level crossing or where there was a river bridge you would find these pill-
> boxes. The bridges, there were bridges all over the place, crossing the drains and
> the rivers, they were immediately all mined. I don't mean they had explosives
> straight away but at the approach to the bridge on either side they took about
> four holes in the road and just filled them with hard core, so if you wanted to
> put a bit of explosives in it was only a few minutes' job to take that loose stuff
> out and charge it with explosives.

People's memories do not attach exact dates to events such as the arrival of pill
boxes. A clue comes in a court case that nearby Skegness, at least for the first
weeks of the summer invasion scare, was as open to the sea as in peacetime. In
an undated case heard on 14 June, a magistrate and special constable, Mr Chester,
was walking with a friend on the beach, when they saw a soldier climbing out

A peacetime view of Skegness front and clock tower on the Lincolnshire coast. According to a
June 1940 court case, two men walking on the beach saw a soldier climbing out of a lock-up shop
underneath the pier. The thief was jailed. The story suggests that weeks after the first fear of invasion,
Skegness was without beach defences.

The West Cliff at Bournemouth. To the west at Dartmouth, the journalist Douglas Reed 'looked down on a placid, empty sea, and on deserted, open, undefended coasts'.

of a lock-up shop underneath the pier. They handed him over to police, and the thief went to prison. So there was nothing to stop people walking on the beach – or coming ashore.

Beach defences did come, but according to the journalist Douglas Reed, on the south coast, for months 'you could walk for miles [on cliffs and beaches] without seeing a soul … The newspapers and the radio had much to say about the great defensive preparations that were being made on the east coast; here, was nothing.'

Ronald Knight , an evacuee from Portsmouth, recalled Upwey near Weymouth: 'On the beach all access to the sea was blocked off by long lines of barbed wire and scaffolding to stop or at least delay any invading enemy forces.' Rob Marshall was at Shanklin on the Isle of Wight: 'As children of a seaside resort we spent all day every day on the beach and at that time beaches were closed, it was like shutting off half of our life.'

Another islander, Les Russell, was a plumber's apprentice turning seventeen in 1940, nicknamed Plumb by the other Home Guards at Chillerton, between Newport and Chale.

> We used to do our training at the Chillerton School, in their playground, Sunday morning … we did our discipline training, sloping arms, and marching and all the rest of it and we did training along hedgerows and digging trenches and making these tank traps, with these oil drums.

The men would roll the drums on to the roads in case tanks came: 'It was primitive.' Each evening the volunteers would 'do two hours outside, there were six of us, two of us used to be outside for an hour and we used to gradually change over, looking out towards the sea. That was in the LDV … We had a .303 rifle, which was one between six of us.'

Across the Solent, Portsmouth's commander, Admiral Sir William James, in a memo dated 14 July summarised the vessels available to the enemy: 24 train ferries which could carry 20 to 30 tanks each; 800 to 1000 barges; fast motor boats; and fishing craft. British naval measures were a patrol of anti-submarine vessels

Concertina wire along the sea front at Sandgate, near Folkestone in Kent. It did not amount to much, although land-mines planted on the beach would be out of sight. (War Office official photograph by Len Puttnam, 10 July 1940)

10–15 miles from shore; destroyer searches at night towards the enemy coast; an inshore patrol within five miles of shore by small craft either side of the Isle of Wight; and mine sweeping trawlers, which swept the Channel by day, and went on observation patrol between the two by night. Les Russell and his elders watching the coast would not mistake their own ships for the enemy, as no merchant vessels were allowed within three miles of the coast between sunset and sunrise without permission.

Portsmouth and nearby Newhaven, Shoreham, Littlehampton, Southampton, Poole, Portland and Bridport were ready to be 'immobilised' if they were likely to fall into enemy hands and parts of south coast piers had been removed or prepared for blowing up.

LONDON

In one of his first notes as Prime Minister, dated 11 May, Churchill asked via Ismay how Whitehall was guarded against parachutists landing on Horse Guards Parade and St James' Park – on his doorstep. It was not a sign, as with some others, of a man fearing for his own safety; rather, it was the query of someone who all his life could not resist poking his nose into military business.

After a telephone call to local Army commanders, the answer was that one company from Regent's Park barracks was at 30 minutes notice, two platoons from the Tower of London likewise, one 'emergency platoon' from Wellington Barracks at 15 minutes notice; and the sentries at Buckingham Palace and St James' Palace armed with ball ammunition. On the one hand, a few hundred parachutists dropped on central London would outnumber the defenders; on the other, you could hardly reinforce landmarks in case of an attack while the battle was on the Continent. Civil servants responded characteristically by making a list. A Treasury report to the War Office on 30 May named six buildings of 'first order of importance', which housed the most vital ministries and headquarters in Whitehall and elsewhere.

A list however is never the same as action. On 23 June Ismay wrote to General Paget.

> The Prime Minister is taking an active interest in the defence arrangements for the Whitehall area and I confess that I am not altogether happy about them. A defence plan of a sort has been made and a number of posts constructed. Each Ministry has caged itself in and installed a guard. The Admiralty have got Royal Marines, the War Office have Guards, the Air Ministry have airmen, this office and others have LDVs. I should have thought that to get satisfactory results the whole area ought to be treated as a defended locality and should be manned by a homogenous unit (if this is possible) and under one commander ... as it is I feel that there is a waste of manpower and no likelihood of co-ordinated action in face of attack.

Paget, the man in military charge locally, answered that the best solution was to close Whitehall to the public and provide such a 'homogenous unit', with small guards at various ministries and a central reserve. Wheels turned; Paget sent a copy to the London area commander, Lieutenant-General Sir Bertram Sergison-Brooke. On 27 June Ismay told Paget that he had had a talk with Sergison-Brooke and that he was 'in a position to answer any conundrums that the Prime Minister may put to me. As you know he takes rather a personal interest in the matter.' This was Ismay's diplomatic way of saying he was taking stick from Churchill, and he commended the other commanders doing their job so that they did not get stick too.

On 23 July (more than two months after Churchill had asked) Ismay informed Churchill that he had studied the scheme of defence and 'it appears to be well thought out and complete.' As for Churchill's idea of giving Whitehall's defence to the Royal Marines, that would require 500 men and it was difficult to find rooms for them in central London. Churchill still stuck his oar in. Also in mid-July, he asked why work on an anti-tank obstacle across St James' Park had stopped. Paget replied that he ordered work stopped a few days before. Instead he proposed two concrete pill-boxes in St James' Park and a belt of wire across the park to prevent access by the enemy 'or fifth column snipers' to the east end of the park over-looking Horse Guards Parade.

One of Churchill's new ministers, Hugh Dalton, described mid-May 1940 in his memoirs as 'tense days'. Everyone, he claimed, expected the German air force to have 'a real go' at Whitehall and Westminster – an attempt at invasion or at least a heavy raid by paratroops: 'Live each day as though the last was then the rule of life for all.'

As everywhere, volunteers filled the gaps. Henry (later Lord) Colyton, a pre-war diplomat working in 1940 as a private secretary, joined his workplace LDV 'at once'.

> To begin with we just wore an armband with LDV on it. Later when we became the Home Guard we were issued with khaki drill, very cold when we were on the Foreign Office roof in an air raid looking out for incendiaries. Rifles and bayonets were kept at the Foreign Office. With our khaki fore and aft forage caps we looked a pretty rugged lot as we were taught to charge down a stretch of grass on the St James's Park side and bayonet sacks of straw, giving a good grunt as the blade went home.

A BIG COUNTRY

London was the biggest city, but most of the country was not London, and men were finding how hard it was to cover all their country against a sea and air invader. At Claverley in Shropshire, a local British Legion meeting – inevitably at the Crown Inn clubroom – divided the parish into twenty. Ten men to a section, each section would have a car and a local resident with a 'telephone installation'. The vicarage would take all telephone messages. Church bells would give the necessary warning.

'I know well that everything possible is being done and I am not for a moment grumbling,' wrote Birdwood to Dill, on 18 September on Guards Club note-paper. It was a sure sign that Birdwood, a 74-year-old Field Marshal of the First World War, *was* grumbling.

> … if anything can be done to expedite equipment for the Home Guard in country districts it will be well worthwhile. I am <u>daily</u> assaulted with complaints re shortages of rifles, ammunition, waterproof sheets and greatcoats. I find many of these men have not yet fired a single round. That is essential but of course we must keep all but a very small amount of ammunition in hand for real use.

Birdwood closed: 'Do not answer this but I feel these things are more essential in county districts than in the big towns.' He was merely passing on a point – the previous day, he had addressed 250 Home Guards at Shepton Mallet. As he wrote, 'Without a rifle a man it is not easy to arrange distribution as men are <u>very</u> scattered and must have their rifles with them.'

CHURCH BELLS

Even the basic method of warning of an invasion, ringing church bells, was crude, all or nothing. The mid-war film *Went The Day Well?* showed this neatly. In the film Germans dressed as British soldiers arrive in a southern English village, to hold an important point ahead of the main invaders. Rumbled, the Germans herd the villagers into the parish church. The old vicar rebels and begins ringing the church bells, only to be shot dead. The village's Home Guards, ironically on a Sunday morning exercise in the country, hear the first bells but think nothing of it, only to be shot dead cycling home.

What did a church bell when rung mean exactly? That someone had spotted parachutists? Or had the next village rung their bell? A Lincolnshire conference of police superintendents in December 1940 noted that the orders about calling out the Home Guard and ringing the church bells had been amended several times. The position by then was to ring bells only for signalling arrival of parachute troops: '... on this summons the local Home Guard will turn out'. Bell-ringing was not to be repeated if parachutes were not seen descending; unless the military commander so ordered.

Something that did send a signal of sorts for miles, which bridged and yet highlighted the gap between town and country, was the night bombing of cities. The volunteers of Binsted in Hampshire, on watch from the church tower as early as 6 June, logged lights to the south in the direction of Portsmouth, and realised it was an air raid. Regularly the watchers reported searchlights on the south coast and, they believed, gun fire from Portsmouth, Southampton and London. Bill Goodwin was then a seventeen-year-old farm worker and Home Guard in the village of Bradley, near Stafford.

We had got a look-out post on top of Bradley Church; you could see right across to Cannock Chase, right the way to the Potteries, Wolverhampton and Birmingham; and with a pair of glasses you could pick no end of buildings out. Coventry is a little bit further along, but of course the raids took place at night … It was like the rising sun, man, really like the rising sun; and every bomb that went in, up went a load of sparks, big sparks, it was horrible. It had got me that interested, because I happened to be on duty for the first half of the night, because there was four of us on, did half the night and two the other half of the night, two o'clock change-over, if I remember right. And I was watching this and I couldn't believe what I was seeing, I just couldn't believe it. And I was so struck by it I didn't even go down at two o'clock, it was four, half past four before I went down for a couple of hours' sleep before I went to work again. The following night I couldn't help it, I had to go up again, and went for four or five hours, the second night.

In the Potteries, the Trentham platoon had its first air raid alert on 24 June. The guard stood-to, with a total firepower of two rifles with ten rounds of ammunition; 'we were all very much on our toes and expecting some activity at any moment'. Alerts followed for the next few days 'and we had an awe-inspiring view of fires and searchlights from the direction of Birmingham.'

While history has shown that the Germans flew over only to bomb, Hugh Tweedie, a retired Admiral and Home Guard battalion commander on the outskirts of Bristol, recalled that air attacks on the city were 'always a source of anxiety to the Home Guard, as it seemed certain then that sooner or later one of those attacks would be the overture for airborne landings on a big scale.' Derrick Hill, a young Home Guard in Much Wenlock in Shropshire, thought similarly.

I was on top of Wenlock Edge and could see a lot of the fires; we saw the bombardment of Coventry, and of Birmingham, when planes were going across to Liverpool, the German planes we could hear them going across at night. And coming back. That didn't help things at all, you thought, perhaps there would be paratroopers in those.

Swathes of England, then, heard or saw the glow of the German invader, even if the Nazis were only dropping bombs, not people. The Battle of Britain and the bombing 'blitz' of the winter of 1940–1 was only in the air, but was a constant reminder of a possible land invasion. Life itself seemed suspended. Douglas Reed stopped trying to write anything; 'Who could write, until he knew the answer to the great question that the future held?' he explained later.

Len Francis, the Cheltenham Grammar School boy whose father was the police sergeant in the Cotswold village of Winchcombe, recalled November 1940. 'The night Coventry was bombed was quite dramatic, we could hear wave after wave of planes passing overhead and could see a glow in the sky to the northeast, I remember my father saying "some poor devils are getting it tonight".'

How much sympathy did Sergeant Francis feel for the distant townspeople? Could anyone not present imagine what it was like to be bombed? Did villagers feel part of the struggle, seeing the war on their landscape, or did the remoteness of it only make them feel less involved? In something as violent and large as a world war it is easy to concentrate on the 'action', whereas for much of the time, in many places, little or nothing warlike happened. So it was in England in 1940, and an effort to learn how the British people imagined invasion will bring us closer to the truth.

CHAPTER 6

IMAGINED INVASION

Every self-respecting man should, with a plan of the city he lives in, practise schemes for an insurrection in times of war or trouble, and for its defence should an insurrection ever come about.
Alan Sillitoe, *Road to Volgograd*, 1964

That was a strange thing for a writer visiting Russia in the 1960s to write. It made a little more sense because as a boy in his native wartime Nottingham, Sillitoe had a self-confessed 'passion for things military'. He read manuals for the Home Guard about tactics and street fighting; he had heard about the previous war from his father and uncles. Much of what men say or do in wartime is down to imagination – and how far they anticipate the worst. Guards in the dark had to identify whether sounds were being made by animals, locals or enemy invaders. The more fertile the guard's imagination, the more on edge he became and the more likely he was to assume that every rustle of leaves was a German paratrooper. At Lewsey on the outskirts of Luton at night, one patroller recalled, sheep coughing sounded very human. Hedgehogs moving noisily through dead leaves; bull frogs croaking, owls hooting, electric cables sparking and fiercely cracking in the drizzle; all tended to fray the nerves of the inexperienced sentry. 'In addition he had to listen to bombs falling on Luton and to speculate on their nearness to his loved ones.'

Similarly Stan Burke – the Shenstone, Staffordshire teenage Home Guard – recalled men tramping around the lanes at night 'and a fox made a noise going through a hedge.' A Home Guard fired at it: 'I think they were expecting parachutists.' Bill Mycock, the Derbyshire Peak farmer and Home Guard, remembered fondly the time when a guard asked men to cover him while he went and had a look at a suspect – a postbox on a tree stump. 'I was almost flat, laughing,' Reginald Titt on the outskirts of Salisbury recalled the weather was good

... and night and dawn duty in the countryside was not unpleasant. It was, nevertheless, a strange experience, to be out in the quiet night, no sign of a light anywhere nor sounds of traffic, except the occasional steam trains on the Southern and Great Western lines through Wilton, about three miles away. Our night vision became very well adapted and we could see quite well but after a while the strain of watching for what might be a real enemy began to tell and it became hard to be sure whether a clump of nettles, that one could only just see, really was stationary or whether it had moved and might be an intruder.

With only five rounds of ammunition, the temptation was to shoot first, then look.

Hollywood offered advice too late for the nerve-jangling months of 1940. At the cinema *Invasion* was showing by the spring of 1942, described in the papers as 'the sensational film of interest to every Britisher. Grim American prophecies of what invasion of Britain will be like ... an amazing film of America's view of our chances of beating off a Nazi attack by sea and air.' A better known wartime film devoted to a fictional invasion – *Went the Day Well?* – reached regional cinemas in spring 1943. Filmmakers sought to give their audience a good story rather than instruction. The length of the filmmaking process meant of course that none could have been ready in 1940. The Ministry of Information did bring out a short instructional film, *Miss Grant goes to the Door*, billed as 'a dramatic telling of what to do in regard to invasion and parachutists.' Free to view, any club or factory could screen it.

Speculation about how to thwart invaders was a gift to the eccentric, such as the vicar of Lutton cum Eysey, Cricklade, S. Claude Tickell. One of the (regular) letters he sent to his local paper asked if every householder could be supplied with a 'harmless soporific ... wherewith to drug parachutists' drinks'. All over the country village, town and workplace commanders imagined how they ought to resist. Major Reginald Green drew a plan for the defence of the Northamptonshire village of Irchester on the back of two cards of a shoe shop's stock list. Many men, like Green, mapped the problem. A village or any place would have several ways in, and depending on neighbouring forces, an attack from one direction could be more dangerous than another. Green noted that 'Static defence should in my opinion be resorted to only in a state of extremity, which means the vacating of outposts and positions advantageous to the holders and moreover cutting ourselves off entirely from outside.' If the Germans attacked from the east, Green and his men would be on their own; if not, their battalion might be able to rescue them. That was worth bearing in mind beforehand.

Some men, in public at least, responded to the threat of invasion with bravado. A Bridgnorth Home Guard, asked by an officer what he would do if German airmen landed, reportedly replied: 'Well, sir, I would bring the dead bodies and put them on your doorstep.' Some were honest. Cyril Turner, who turned eighteen in 1940, recalled the German bombing of Yarmouth when the sky was so clear you could see the planes.

> Our commander paid a visit during the night, to make sure we were alert. He said to my friend, 'what steps would you take if you saw the Hun come down in parachutes?' 'Bloody long ones', he said.

Men struggled to visualise how to beat the German weapons – the dive-bomber and the tank. The poet Cecil Day Lewis, looking back in a newspaper article on the first eight months of his Home Guard experience in his unidentified 'little patch of England' in south Devon, recalled a night exercise. An enemy tank 'represented by our window-cleaner's push-bike and sidecar was lying up for the night in an orchard off the road. Four of us were with the tank, the rest of us had to attack it.' Day Lewis had rigged up a trip wire with tin cans giving the 'tank crew' warning of approaching attackers and giving them time to move off, but the crew were 'chivvied all over the countryside … We could not pass through a gate or a gap without having bombs (flour bags filled with sawdust) chucked at us.'

The Army also used role play to predict potential German tactics and plan how to combat them. A 'special correspondent' of *The Times*, inside the combined operations room of Lieutenant-General Auchinleck at Southern Command in October, reported a war game. War Office officers acted as the German general staff.

> The general from his raised platform looks down upon a huge inch map of the whole area and can take in the position at a glance in the event of operations. Each beach is numbered on the map, the position of mobile reserves and blockhouses marked and there are coloured tokens for ships, dive bombers, parachutists and tanks waiting to be moved.

Who could say whether the Germans had any other weapons at hand? Lack of information led to outlandish reports. On 22 June, Northamptonshire passed on intelligence that the enemy might spray from aircraft 'corrosive acid', or shoot acid from armoured fighting vehicles (AFVs). Men could readily detect the acid, the report went on helpfully, 'by a burning sensation on the skin or burning effect on clothing or vegetation'. One newspaper columnist wondered if Hitler had a new trick, such as 'emergency floats like balloon tyres' for troop-carrying planes, to land in some shallow estuary.

The wilder imaginings were stimulated partly by the German use of paratroopers in May 1940, which to both to the public and military mind seemed almost insane. Today we forget how revolutionary the tactic was, but it meant that there appeared to be no limit to what the Nazis might try. A letter to a Sutton Coldfield newspaper signed only 'W' suggested stretching wires or cables across

Sutton Park on the outskirts of Birmingham, in case troops landed. 'We are deal-ing with madmen ready and eager to fling their lives away and the opportunity may soon be here for them to make mass flights.' There was similar panic higher up. Appended to a minute by Churchill in mid-July, the First Sea Lord noted a 'characteristic of the Hitler regime'. You could not assume that past military rules 'as to what is practicable or what is impracticable will be allowed to govern the action taken'. Not only had Hitler embraced new methods of making war, but the British feared that the dictator would risk losses that Allied generals would regard as a defeat, in order to achieve his goals.

CHANNEL TEST FLIGHT

The military had to answer some 'what-ifs' in a hurry – would British radar detect gliders approaching? How far inland might a paratroop glider travel? The wrong answer or the wrong tactics in response to the threat, and England could lose the war. On 6 June a committee for the Scientific Survey of Air Warfare considered the possibility of invasion by enemy troops towed at night in gliders behind aircraft, and released at 10,000 feet to glide in silently and undetected. The committee recommended trials at Swanage. The committee quoted a New British Broadcasting Station (that is, Nazi propaganda) broadcast of 28 May stat-ing that the Germans might land troops by gliders. The committee thought it 'not impossible' that the enemy could land anything up to 10,000 men without warn-ing within a few hours at night. And as for the enemy not being likely to reveal his plan over the radio, the committee noted that the NBBS might be conveying information and instructions to Fifth Column agents in Britain, or the enemy was double-bluffing. On 9 June, Downing, in charge of Fighter Command, asked Air Vice Marshal R.H. Peck at the Air Ministry if he had any information about the very large tank-carrying aircraft which were 'unreliably reported to be under construction in the Black Forest'.

On 12 June a man with glider experience, Wing Commander G.M. (Mungo) Buxton, of the School of Aeronautical Engineering, Henlow, at Swanage, asked for several expert glider pilots. The first test flight due on Saturday 22 June was spoiled, as was the Sunday, by low cloud. The next day a training aircraft took a glider 21.5 miles out to sea – well within sight of the enemy coast – to 10,000 feet, and released it. The glider returned successfully. The trial found radar was 'reasonably' able to detect gliders. Buxton reported from his special duty flight at Christchurch that gliders, released at 10,000 feet, had a range of 25 miles. That meant gliders could land up to ten miles inland, tallying with how far into France the American and British paratroopers landed on D-Day.

The Deputy Chief of Air Staff, Air Vice Marshal Douglas, told his fellow senior RAF officers on 24 July that Germany probably had 1,000 glider pilots. The enemy had used gliders in Belgium on a limited scale. A number of gliders could land close together in twilight or moonlight, meaning up to 100 of the enemy with automatic weapons, in a body. They might try to seize an aerodrome near a port as a bridgehead – again, not unlike the British paratroops on D-Day, who secured bridges.

Douglas put the coastal strip at risk at 15–20 miles deep. It was fortunate that radar could detect gliders 'since even in daylight they [the south coast experiments] have escaped the notice of the Observer Corps.' More tests followed, arguably some of the bravest Royal Air Force flying of the summer. On 8 July for example, a tug and unarmed glider saw eight enemy aircraft, but accepted the risk without comment because of the need to complete the tests quickly.

ON THE CONTINENT

On the continent was the place to learn what the Germans intended, but people there had no way to pass their findings on to Britain. In 1944 South Somerset Home Guard invited to their headquarters a 1940 British prisoner of war from Calais.

> He recounted how on one occasion the prisoners were ordered to remove quantities of waste paper from the officers' quarters of a crack German regiment. The paper consisted of torn up maps. Some of our men secreted pieces about their clothing and on return to camp reassembled the fragments after the fashion of a jigsaw puzzle. The maps were of southern England.

William Shirer, the Berlin-based American newspaper and radio man, was doing his best to report the truth about Nazi Germany, or at least not repeat its propaganda. Late in the summer of 1940 the Germans took him on a tour of – so he was told – the invasion fleet. Shirer believed the Germans were bluffing and did not do a (censored) broadcast as the Germans wished – but other reporters, who put a scoop ahead of their scruples, did.

FACE TO FACE

The general staff's job was to put their best guesses on paper. On 15 August, weighing up the east and south coasts, they talked up the danger to the south coast – though the Straits of Dover would be a 'dangerous bottleneck' for the invader. It would depend on the Germans gaining air superiority, and 'the denial of the Channel to British naval forces'. A September intelligence summary said that the sandy beaches between Folkestone and Hastings would be easier to land on than the east Kent cliffs. But such an attack might be a feint, with the main attack at Harwich.

Civilians, knowing none of this, had to go by what they read in the papers and heard on the radio or through gossip. A widely-printed newspaper column about pet dogs ('Tail-Wagger Talks' by Philokuon) in June 1940 quoted a friend 'who has influence in high quarters' who rang to ask Philokuon if dogs were of use against enemy parachutists. The writer answered that in rural districts, dogs would warn their owners if unauthorised people were about. He recounted stories of parachutists in Rotterdam demanding food from houses at the point of revolvers. There was, so Philokuon claimed, a danger of 'burglarious demands in the dark hours'.

What would become of people? Public anti-Nazis feared the worst. Reginald Titt recalled that as a student before the war he was active in left-wing politics, 'and had grounds for believing myself to have been on the lists of right wing organisations, probably with photographs taken at demonstrations. I had little expectation of survival if we lost the war.' Miss F.L. Josephy – Hampstead resident, president of the National League of Young Liberals, prospective parliamentary candidate for Devizes – told a Highgate audience: 'I would be shot if any number of Germans got here and Gestapo rule was established.' That was, she went on, because she had spoken against Hitler and Nazism, and she was prepared to be killed. 'Should such people be prepared to carry on underground?' she asked. To some, reading this in the local newspapers, it sounded like boasting. One letter writer replied sarcastically about 'meetings in the best drawing rooms in Hampstead to discuss how to change the world', and suggested Miss Josephy parachute into German territory as an agent.

Young men, in particular, sought to prepare themselves for the possible trials ahead. Don Evans was sixteen when he joined the LDV in Salisbury, no questions asked about his age.

> At first we were sorted out in twos and threes with most of us young kids put with a couple of older men. Our principal job was to patrol the open country looking for parachutists. It was generally considered that, if a parachutist could be taken before he had the chance to get organised, he would be easy meat. What would have happened if we really did meet one, I dread to think. My partner with a 12 bore shotgun and me with the latest thing in cudgels doesn't bear thinking about.

Most of Evans' patrolling was on the higher ground outside the city,

> … and only once did something happen to break the routine. I was with Phil Phillips and we were making our way up to the top of Laverstock Downs to relieve Sailor Churchill and Dusty Miller. Looking towards the south we could see that Southampton was being blitzed. We had just met the other two when

an aircraft flew over making a strange noise. It was obviously in trouble and did in fact crash in flames a couple of miles away somewhere in the Pitton area. Suddenly Phil shouted, 'Look, a parachute'. We pushed a round up the breach, lifted the safety catch and ran towards the parachutist. We need not have worried. He was a young lad of around my age; he had landed in the middle of a thorn bush and was covered in scratches. He was crying and had messed himself. He was convinced he would be shot. He spoke good English and was able to tell us he was the only survivor from the aircraft. We handed him over to the police … I must confess, I had always been afraid of the Germans. I always imagined them to be 17-stone, six-and-a-half footers with a square head and an iron fist. Seeing this young lad in front of me snivelling and stinking did me good. I was no longer afraid of Germans.

Another German prisoner was not as A.G. Street imagined, either. Street and his Wiltshire village Home Guard had been part of a hunt for an airman. They went to the police station to see the man, who had 'a curious dignity about him'.

I was dead keen to hunt that fellow, felt the exhilaration as I did when hunts were running and would have shot him on the instant if need be. But somehow when he was caught I had no further quarrel with him.

From the Rolleston and Stretton Home Guard exercise, June 1941: a rifleman escorts a 'prisoner' – who still is carrying his bayonet by his side.

REHEARSALS

What if you saw a German coming your way? Railwaymen and other workers had to know how to deny the enemy use of machinery, such as steam engines. Joe Lakin in 1940 was a 23-year-old locomotive fireman out of Burton-on-Trent.

> At the time of Dunkirk we were expecting to be invaded. Railwaymen were instructed to the effect that if you saw a parachutist you were to take the regulator off and immobilise the engine and clear off. Take a fortnight to take it off – hadn't seen them off since it was made. These were the ludicrous things they told you to do.

And if a German was coming up your garden path? Did you hide? Run? These were basic questions in 1940. In June a Hinckley hosiery hand told his workmates that he would do nothing. The man found himself in court on an 'alarm and despondency' charge – magistrates fined him the huge sum of £20 for being defeatist. What probably counted most against him was saying that the country should be suing for peace.

Hugh Tweedie, the Somerset Home Guard battalion commander, reminisced how before the war he could drive 50 miles to Lyme Regis after breakfast, bathe and return home for tea. It was not so far a distance, he realised, as to prevent the Germans cutting off the south-west from the rest of England. Yet the 'Battle of Bewdley' and many other over-reactions showed that people were if anything too quick to use their imagination. Could they even recognise an invader? This was not as daft as it may sound. Even veterans of 1914–18 had seldom seen their enemy. A leaflet 'If the Invader Comes' told people who saw anything suspicious to try and check the facts, and report to the military or police. An example was given of what kind of information should be imparted:

> At 5.30pm tonight I saw 20 cyclists come into Little Squashborough from the direction of Great Mudtown. They carried some sort of automatic rifle or guns. I did not see anything like artillery. They were in grey uniforms.

With so little to go on, men like the Home Guards rehearsed encounters with the invader in their heads and among themselves. This led to the accidental death of a sixteen-year-old Oratory School, Caversham boy. The inquest heard that the school's officer training cadets handed the boy ten rounds of ammunition for a patrol. One of the other boys took the rifle. The dead boy was armed with a cane. This effort by teachers to keep the rifle and ammunition apart did not work. A third boy told the court that the boy who fired the shot had been fooling around, parrying and lunging at the imaginary enemy.

THE POLICE: A DILEMMA

The duty of police in the event of invasion raised a 'very difficult question', as Churchill admitted, in a 3 August minute to the Lord Privy Seal and Home Secretary, forwarding a memo by his old Liberal colleague Lord Mottistone. Churchill was against the police being forced to follow German orders in an invaded area. In principle, he wrote, the police should withdraw from the area with the last troops, the same for the ARP, fire fighters and other official bodies. That way, men in uniform would be available to fight on in other areas, but it would mean forcing them to leave their families behind. Would the government order them to do so? So difficult was the question the authorities avoided it. It would be impossible for uniformed officials to remain in occupied territory without being forced to become the enemy's servant, and if a policeman tried to aid the free part of England, the occupiers would regard him as a uniformed enemy. By this time, the Germans were occupying the Channel Islands. Police, post offices and so on there were serving the occupier, because there was no prospect of throwing the Germans out. When the English recaptured any invaded place, would those temporarily under the Germans, even if only for a day or a week, have clear consciences?

In an enemy occupation, the bulk of the police were under orders to withdraw. A rearguard would assist the authorities and guard against agents making contact with the enemy, then the rearguard would withdraw too. If there had been no time for civilians to evacuate, that rearguard would be, if possible, made up of men over military service age and those whose families were not evacuated.

The memo dated 7 September, 'Duties of police in case of invasion' by the Home Secretary, went on to say of those left behind: 'Their instructions should be to ensure that the civil population conform to any orders which may have been issued e.g. as to remaining where they are and generally to do everything in their power to assist the civil authorities and the civilians who remain.'

People felt more secure once they had concrete orders, but during the summer months constables were left to wonder. The twenty-year-old Metropolitan Police probationer Mike Crossley recalled in his memoirs of wartime: 'There were no plans on what we should do when this [invasion] happened and it was worrying.'

Nor was it only the lowliest constables who were worrying. Writing to a Stormont civil servant in February 1942, the Royal Ulster Constabulary's Deputy Inspector-General, Major C.F.F. Davies, could not say whether he had had all Home Office circulars dealing with invasion. The RUC had asked Stormont what were the duties of police in an invasion, in a file dated August 1940, but never had a reply. Davies ended diplomatically: 'I think the policy to be adopted in event of invasion is one for discussion.'

What if police in areas still in British hands caught looters, suspected spies, or other criminals? Instead of the usual justice there would be 'war zone courts', at county halls or such central locations. The handful of picked magistrates, hearing short-cut trials, sound sinisterly secretive. Yet if Herefordshire is anything to go by, working people might have found war zone courts more friendly – free of robes and with a balance of trade unionist and Labour magistrates – compared with peacetime, when almost all the county's magistrates were Tories.

FLIGHT OR FIGHT?

As one exchange of views shows, Churchill was setting the tone for resistance, yet at the same time the officials beneath him were not settling the details. The Bristol regional commissioner's office wrote to the Home Office enclosing a letter from Gloucestershire County Council clerk Richard Moon, asking if local government officers should stay at their posts, or go home and destroy all evidence.

The reply on 8 July was that local government should stay put, because the enemy was likely to use the staff, 'and it is better that the civil population in areas occupied by the enemy should deal with our own people'. The regional commissioner would retreat in the face of the enemy and might have to withdraw from the region altogether. The Home Office gave as a reason the (unlikely) possibility that the enemy would wish to employ regional commissioners or their staffs. It looked like one rule for higher officials and another for the rest.

Moon replied to Bristol on 16 July that Gloucestershire's county (civil defence) controller was not prepared to act on what Bristol had called 'an unofficial expression of opinion' from Whitehall. Gloucester called for an official ruling. Meanwhile, Gloucestershire County Council prepared to evacuate council staff that could be of assistance to the military and civilians in unoccupied parts of the county.

Bristol forwarded the letter to the Ministry of Home Security, adding the disclaimer, 'This is typical of the attitude of the clerks of this county council.' On 26 July George Chrystal of the Ministry of Health wrote to Home Security that Gloucestershire's county council chairman and clerk had visited him to make the point that in a town it would be a municipal duty to carry on, but if the county town was falling to the enemy, part of the county council should go while the going was good, to carry on administration in the rest of the county. The clerk quoted Churchill's 'dictum' about fighting street to street, then challenged Churchill to think harder. Should local Home Guards fight to the last cartridge, then retire to their desks, to carry on administration under German orders? Chrystal replied, 'with all deference and reserve … that the Prime Minister's words were rather to be taken as an expression of the country's unanimous determination than as a definite programme of official action'. Chrystal however did admit later that Gloucester had a point. Was Chrystal thinking whether he might have to carry on under the Germans? As officials wrote in the same file, a reserve position had attractions for carrying on the fight, but an 'exodus at a critical moment' would not look good.

STAYING PUT

If police and (some) officials could flee, why not anyone else? The military would not like civilians getting in the way on the roads, let alone in a battle. Anyone outdoors after an invasion risked death from bombs or poison gas. Running away was irrational – how could you tell one place was safer than another? 'Many women, wives and daughters of the Home Guard, write saying can I advise them how to get away to a safe place and can I persuade their husbands to go too,' John Langdon-Davies wrote in one of his Sunday newspaper columns. 'There are no safe places.' A basic urge was at work; if a battle was coming close, people would run the other way, no matter how sensible the official advice to 'stay put'.

Hugh Meynell was at prep school in 1940 when his father joined the LDV in Albrighton in Shropshire. His father said that if the Germans came, the family would go to relations in Yarm. And yet, as Meynell recalled: 'One saw these frightening pictures on the newsreels and of refugees fleeing away with nothing but the clothes they stood up in, a very frightening scenario; and the Germans were pretty beastly, their Stuka bombers were bombing women and children indiscriminately.' Nevertheless, his father was prepared to risk a drive north-east, across an invaded country, in the hope of reaching somewhere safer.

Fred Barratt planned on going the opposite way to the Meynells. He was prepared to take his wife Elsie and son Peter about 30 miles east from Wednesfield to his uncle Fred Crew, a grocer at Cleobury Mortimer, who had a spare room. Barrett would have returned to his Home Guard post as soon as possible. If he

Some illustrations from John Langdon-Davies' December 1940 book *The Home Guard Training Manual*: how to dig a weapon pit; the silhouettes of the Junkers 52 troop carrying aircraft; and the silhouettes of the Junkers 87 dive-bomber and Heinkel 111 bomber, for recognition purposes.

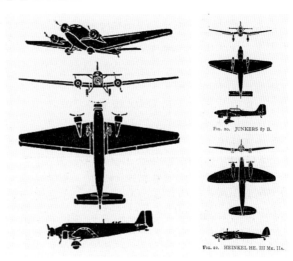

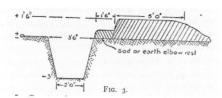

had had warning of invasion, the family would have had food packed and Fred would have sought to borrow a factory van. The authorities did not want roads congested, but Fred naturally wanted his loved ones safe.

> I would have tried to get them away into the country. Even if we had push-biked it, because she [his wife] had a bike with a seat on the back I made, to dangle Peter. We could have made 35 miles.

Fred Barrett had talked it over with a neighbour who had a Ford van who might have evacuated Fred's family.

> If there had been warning, if we had got all night, it should have been possible at night; Bridgnorth would have been the main difficulty, with the bridge; I would have put my uniform on and stood a good chance. We don't know. I know I should have tried to get them away. [His uncle] had got a pretty good petrol allowance, he had an Austin 7 he did his work in. If things looked as though it would happen, he would have come and fetched them and got them out of the way.

Most people who honestly weighed the 'stay put' idea admitted, like Sir Findlater Stewart of the Home Defence Executive, that it would not work, 'however persistent the propaganda'. He saw a difference between staying put when the enemy's line had so far surrounded a town 'that the safest and indeed the only course is for the civil population to stay in their houses, and staying put in an area which seems certain to be the scene of actual hostilities'. He gave the example of Tyneside, that both sides might shell and bomb at the same time. 'Either by the north bank railway or by the roads they [civilians] will try to move up the river to Newcastle. I doubt if anything but shooting will stop them and I doubt also whether the British troops will shoot them.' Could the authorities leave crowds of refugees to be shelled and perhaps driven in front of the enemy as a screen? If not, they should plan for clearing away

Bridges over the Tyne at Newcastle. As the authorities anticipated, during an invasion crowds of refugees might be driven in front of the enemy as a screen, or get in the way of troops using the main roads. The Newcastle 'Fortress' commander Colonel J.L.C. White of Fenham barracks repeated national policy to Team Valley industrial estate tenants at a September 1940 meeting: civilians should *stay put* during fighting. But would they?

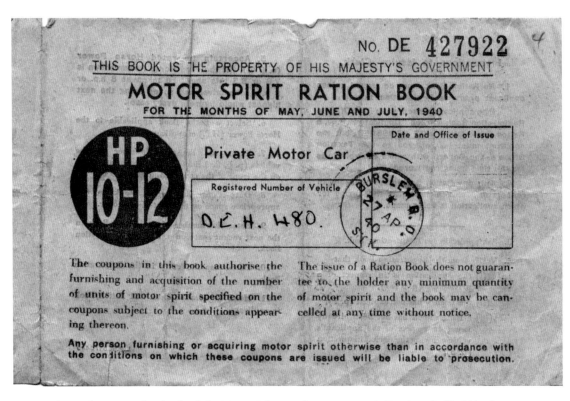

A page from a petrol ration book for May to July 1940 for a car owner in Burslem, Staffordshire. It was feared that paratroopers might seize cars or lorries on landing.

'large congregations of refugees', although that should be secret and the stay put policy should 'hold the field'. No wonder the authorities avoided giving straight answers about what people should do in an invasion.

People had already proved they would not stay put. Fear of bombing from the air when war broke out, though unfounded, led to thousands fleeing London for the south coast – ironically, by midsummer 1940, an invasion-facing coast. Then, as one weekly paper's diarist began rather sourly, 'the wanderers' returned, in time for several months of bombing.

DREAMS

Given that so many people avoided the what-ifs of 1940 as too unpleasant, it is not surprising that some looked back on that summer as unreal. In a Warwickshire Home Guard unit history, an unnamed Rugby School man wrote that he would never forget dawn over the Rumbrook valley; nor midnight vigils in the orderly room: '… a picture of Rugby at war nonetheless vivid because it was a war which never really happened'. Another unit historian, well before the end of the war, fired a litany of questions:

It is difficult to recapture the real emotions of 1940. Already the picture has faded and men's inmost thoughts are locked in their hearts. They will not say what they felt and would not at the time, they were shy to do so; they did not wish to add to their comrades' burden by wild talk and hazardous guesses. Posterity will ask how did the ordinary man take it and what did he feel? Was he defiant? Was he afraid? Was he indifferent? Or did he hold the English view that it would all come right in the end?

If people responded to the prospect of invasion – at least in public – with a 'business as usual' attitude, was that because people felt it was best, or expected of them; or was it a failure to take the threat seriously? Local newspapers of 1940 were seldom ones to canvas opinion on the street. One can sense the strain of the Eastbourne reporter trying to fathom how townspeople took the news of the French request for a cease-fire in mid-June – which meant the next stop for the Germans was a south coast town like Eastbourne. 'There were many people on the seafront yesterday,' the *Eastbourne Gazette* reported on 19 June, 'and there was a general air of cheerfulness and calm among them.' What, if anything, was in the minds of the large crowds enjoying the bandstand music? A week before, shells exploded out to sea. Holiday-makers on the beach 'did not trouble to turn their heads'. Were they brave, or foolish?

It took imagination to add Germans to the peaceful landscape, but some managed it well enough, like the Wiltshire writer who recalled how in late 1940 the Home Guard defence was moved into the county town of Trowbridge from a road block outside.

> It was rather a shock. So many of us had pictured ourselves lying, bloody and mutilated corpses at West Ashton crossroads surrounded by hundreds of dead Germans that we had killed single-handed, that it was rather a blow to learn that the venue of the earning of our posthumously awarded VCs was to be altered.

The authorities did try to make the populace aware of how bad the Germans could be, in the hope of making them work and fight harder. W.J. Brown, a former Wolverhampton MP, as a spokesman for the Ministry of Information asked his audience at Bridgnorth town hall to contemplate a German overlord in the town, with soldiers, a local department of the Gestapo, and citizens who had to listen to the wireless in secret, with a blanket over their heads. 'This [is] the Germany of today … there would be no freedom of any kind, of religion, speech or politics.' Neither the speaker nor the reporter dwelled on whether some people might not mind the loss of those freedoms, if they did not care for religion, and if they felt they never had a say in the running of their town and country. And what was the good of freedom to listen to the wireless if you could not afford one? Douglas

Reed heard a small shopkeeper early in the war 'openly say that it did not interest him one way or the other … His life, his business would go on much the same under Hitler.' Reed and the shopkeeper never had the chance to find out if this was true.

There was only the waiting and time for imagining. Joe Bishop, teenage lorry and tractor driver at Brettenham, near Thetford, in the Home Guard like his father:

> We used to have two regular nights in a week, used to sit there, all we had to do is sit and wait for the telephone to ring. Used to read a book or doze in a chair, waiting for it to ring. Of course it never did ring, but we had to be there just in case.

CHAPTER 7

BASIL LIDDELL HART AND GEORGE ORWELL

Basil Liddell Hart – 'military scientist', according to *Who's Who 1943* – faced a dilemma thanks to the German victory in France. He had stated that the more mechanised army would be victorious, and had been proved right. Once the war was safely won he claimed the Germans took his ideas and used them. Yet that actual moment of May 1940 was embarrassing for him. Tellingly, the second volume of his memoirs stopped with the conquest of the west in 1940, which he called 'a world shaking disaster which changed the course of history for the worse. Though never was a great disaster more easily preventable.' Why did Liddell Hart not write about what happened next, to his own country, and himself? Why did he write so little at the time? If he sought to say he was right all along about a more mechanised army, he would be at best a 'told you so' – hardly popular. As things stood, Germany had a continent-conquering mechanised army and the best Britain had was rusting on the Dunkirk beaches, so it looked as if Britain could not win, or at least not until it built a tank army as big as the enemy's. Could it ever? People would hardly thank Hart for pointing this out. Given some of the defeatist talk that had put Englishmen in court in June 1940, Hart had to be careful he did not become a scapegoat. The typescript of his late 1940 book *Dynamic Defence*, his first chance to comment at length on the war, had this line crossed out from the first page: 'Never probably has greater point been given to the particular proverb coined by Britain's foes of the past that her people never knew when they were beaten'. Was Liddell Hart saying Britain was beaten?

This was a man who lived by military ideas – made his living, more to the point, writing about them. A mere seven pages out of the 416 in his 1941 book *The Current of War*, that covered 1940, were about the summer invasion threat. Nor did Liddell Hart make up for quantity with quality. For instance, he discussed the possibility of swimming enemy tanks, and offered a pen-picture of a 'flood' of boats 'belching forth a swarm of armoured reptiles which after making their way ashore could carry out a rapid advance inland'. For a 'military scientist', talk of belching and reptiles was suspiciously inexact, unscientific.

Liddell Hart always liked praise, and he had some even at this low point in his career. After his 18 August article in the *Sunday Pictorial*, Lloyd George told him it was 'the finest I have ever read'. Enttled 'Invasion: RAF will decide our fate', it began with a characteristic call for clear thinking, rather than muddling through. Hart argued Britain would mainly rely on the Royal Navy to repel invasion, but in the south-east where the Channel was narrow, the RAF was most important. He stressed Britain's limited manpower and called for his country to concentrate on air and sea power and a mechanised army, requiring relatively small manpower. He did not mention the Home Guard.

Praise from Lloyd George was no surprise, as Liddell Hart was a guest of his in Wales in the summer of 1940. On 8 May Liddell Hart had declined a salary as Lloyd George's military adviser, preferring to stay 'voluntary'. The approval of Lloyd George was part of Hart's problem. The former Prime Minister liked what Hart was saying because Lloyd George, too, could see no way of winning. That made them dangerous defeatists, according to some. Yet another sign that Hart was out of the loop, even paralysed in 1940, when his country needed him most, is his dismissal of the Home Guard. He had given even less respect to the LDV. Writing in the *News Chronicle* about invasion in mid-June – under the snappy title 'Keep our heads and use them' – he identified the natural urge to do something, such as a levee en masse. But he questioned its usefulness in the days of mechanised warfare. He wanted quality rather than quantity; he wanted people 'to do the right thing rather than something'. Again, Hart was flying in the face of public opinion. Above all, people wanted to do something, anything.

THE REVOLUTIONARY PATRIOT

Someone else who did not make a good name for himself in 1940 was George Orwell, who incidentally after he met Liddell Hart for the first time in September 1942 described him as 'very defeatist'. The summer of 1940 should have been made for a man like Orwell. As a wounded militiaman survivor of the Spanish Civil War, he was one of fairly few left-wingers who knew militarily what he was talking about. And he wanted to talk about it. *Time and Tide* magazine printed a letter of his in June 1940, when he was careful to give his credentials: 'I had a front-seat view of the street fighting in Barcelona in May 1937.'

In a summer when, supposedly, the common danger of German invasion brought people together, Orwell should have thrived. This was a man who had experience of all classes: the old Etonian and imperial policeman in Burma had become a tramp, a reporter, and a socialist. Yet Orwell looked in vain for war work and, until he joined the BBC in 1941, scratched around as a theatre and book reviewer – hardly a contribution to the war effort, as he knew well. He admitted to feeling 'useless'.

He was dead within ten years and by then on his way to becoming the most famous literary Englishman of his time. What then was not going right for Orwell in 1940? Partly, he was a late developer and until the mid-1940s did not quite find the role that suited him, as a Johnsonian essayist and story-teller. Whenever he worked otherwise, as a novelist, poet and newspaper reporter, he was (with some exceptions) unimpressive. Why did other men more or less forgotten since, like John Brophy and John Langdon-Davies, not Orwell, grab the chance to make headlines, and cash, for themselves, as home defence and Home Guard commentators? Orwell would have been glad of the money, and he was as well qualified as anyone. In his 1938 book about the Spanish war, *Homage to Catalonia*, he proved a vivid and insightful writer about revolutionary war, fighting on the side of badly armed and barely trained workers. Orwell began that book with the story of a brief meeting with an Italian fellow volunteer he took an immediate liking to: 'Something in his face deeply moved me.' It moved him, years later, to his finest verse of poetry.

> But the thing that I saw in your face
> No power can disinherit;
> No bomb that ever burst
> Shatters the crystal spirit.

Why did Orwell, in 1940, not feel moved the same as he did in Spain? And when he made it into print, why did he not find much of an audience, as he did with *Animal Farm* and *1984*? Unlike in revolutionary Barcelona in the winter of 1936/7, the English working class was not even for a moment 'in the saddle'. Orwell could sense great change, in need of chronicling – he began a diary on 28 May 1940 as the battle of France turned towards disaster – yet we find him noting advertisements in newspapers. It became material for his book written between August and October 1940 and published in 1941, *The Lion and the Unicorn*. He despised England as 'still the rich man's paradise', yet saw socialism as no more than 'a realisable policy'. Orwell's personal breakthrough, his response to 1940, laid out in this little book, was that England could be – had to be, to beat Hitler, he argued – revolutionary, *and* patriotic: 'By revolution we become more ourselves, not less.'

Whereas Labour Party leaders thought only of compromise, entering the Tory Churchill's Cabinet – admittedly, to prevent something worse, Britain under Hitler – Orwell looked for social conflict. Writing in his diary on 17 September, in London under air raids, he thought of 'St Petersburg in 1916' – that is, a land in wartime turning any month, any week now, to revolution.

Orwell did not have newspaper contacts to give him a mass audience, unlike Brophy or Langdon-Davies. Orwell was chalking 'Sack Chamberlain' on a wall in the summer of 1940, according to a diary entry of 1941, not typing it for a Fleet Street newspaper. Orwell claimed in *The Lion and the Unicorn* that his ideas could be printed on the front page of the *Daily Mirror*. But did the *Daily Mirror* or any other newspaper editor want to suggest, in print, as Orwell did, 'red militia billeted in the Ritz'? What mass market newspaper would dare print what he put in one autumn 1940 magazine article: 'I dare say the London gutters will have to run with blood.' Orwell's thinking was too violent for mainstream newspapers and society to take.

The war had upset his literary concentration so that he could 'only' write journalism, not fiction. He shelved a long novel with the proposed title of *The Lion and the Unicorn*. He let his standards slip: writing reviews, he admitted to his diary on 17 June 1940, he typed his words straight rather than taking any more care by re-writing. For some of his biographers, that was a sign he had come of age as a fluent writer. Yet Orwell did not type *1984* at one go. Surely the truth was a loss of self-respect by someone who had sought for years to make himself a writer, knowing poverty and uncertainty, relying on his writing to pay the bills. Orwell was depressed. He felt his country was going wrong, and had to change, and he cared.

Orwell's criticism was of a 'moneyed class' that he used to belong to. He complained in *The Lion and the Unicorn* that the Home Guard was deliberately organised so only those with private incomes could afford the time and money to be in command. Orwell rose to the rank of sergeant, the highest rank you could in practice take while holding down a job.

The Lion and the Unicorn shows that when he did write about 1940, in 1940, he was on form. Compare Orwell's striking first line of *The Lion and the Unicorn* – 'As I write, highly civilised human beings are flying overhead, trying to kill me' – with the stabs that lesser writers had at a similar idea. That Orwell could humanise the anonymous, dangerous air raid – identifying man to man, though in the dark – was as moving as his hand-shake with the Italian in Spain.

As for the flatter efforts of others, John Langdon-Davies began his book *Fifth Column*, published in August 1940: 'As I write these words, the enemies of civilisation are battering at the gates of Paris. By the time they can be read, it is possible that our own country will already have been defiled by the machines of the invaders.' Stirring, but how many readers would know if they felt 'defiled'? Tom Wintringham in his July 1940 book, selling far more copies than any of Orwell's to date, was urging on readers the personal nature of the threat. He began his book like Orwell, without Orwell's style or insight: 'At the moment when these pages are written, Britain is in danger of invasion by an opponent using new methods of war.'

Strange that Orwell had to resort to a diary. It suggests that he had no paying public outlet for what he wanted to put on paper. As someone who hoped for reds in the Ritz you wonder how Orwell would have stood in an English equivalent of Barcelona in 1937. Would Orwell have been shot as a revolutionary? Would he have been a sergeant giving the firing squad their orders? Or would Orwell, Cromwell-like, have risen in rank in an English revolution?

For a man hailed after his death as someone who was left-wing *and* a champion of his own country – to take the title of his collected works for that year, he was 'a patriot after all' – Orwell in public was extreme, and in private alienated from his countrymen, of all classes. On 25 June according to his diary he put his name down for Home Service battalions.

> The man who took my name etc was the usual imbecile and old soldier with medals of the last war who could barely write. In writing capital letters he more than once actually wrote them upside down.

On 30 June he wrote of an LDV gathering in Regent's Park.

> The general inspecting the parade was the usual senile imbecile, actually decrepit and made one of the most uninspiring speeches I ever heard … The men however very ready to be inspired. Loud cheering at the news that rifles have appeared at last.

For a man who was supposed to identify with the downtrodden, Orwell appeared to view the old illiterate soldier – who was hardly to blame for his Victorian schooling – as no different from the general. Both were an 'imbecile'. Orwell was still grumbling about colonels in notes on the Home Guard he sent to Liddell Hart in 1942.

WELCOME WRITING

Liddell Hart and Orwell were in the literary wilderness in 1940 because the country did not want to be told where they had gone wrong. More welcome was writing that told people what to do next. John Brophy seized the season – and the market – with his book, *Home Guard: A Handbook for the LDV* (1940). Brophy was a veteran of 1914–18 – he ran away from school in 1914 and enlisted before he was fifteen, according to *Who's Who*. In plain English he stressed what men of his generation could do, even if it was something small and brief: 'If the enemy is delayed only an hour that is good work done and the longer the delay the better for the British defence as a whole.' The 'Red Revolutionary' Tom Wintringham, the man who taught the Home Guard guerrilla warfare, by comparison made blunt, political demands for a democratic army. It meant Wintringham was the one forced out of position by conservatives, while Brophy's career writing fact and fiction about the war long prospered.

Liddell Hart complained in private of newcomers as military critics – whereas he was something more, a 'military scientist'. He was the sort of man to draw up a private list of who was correspondent for which Fleet Street paper. If newspapers were employing younger blood with newer ideas than his, whose fault was that? The journalist John Langdon-Davies had felt 'terrified' beneath dive-bombing in Finland, which he called the 'most unpleasant thing in the world'. But Spanish Republican soldiers on the Ebro when dive-bombed had learned to take it, he reminded readers. This was what people queued up to hear. What was it like under a dive bomber? ('Noise is indeed the worst thing in modern warfare.') Half of Langdon-Davies' book *Home Guard Warfare* was the lecture he gave to 100 Home Guard battalions, several hundred men each time, organised by the *Sunday Pictorial* newspaper from November 1940 to April 1941. He had to turn down 400 more requests to speak. Langdon-Davies began *Home Guard Warfare* by recalling how the Spanish Republicans put their heads together to beat tanks and other enemy weapons. Langdon-Davies thought that war would be more professional in England, and that a BBC announcer would explain which way the war was going. That was wrong, he later admitted. The Home Guard built its own barricades.

Britain was unprepared for war, as in the South African War (1899–1902) and 1914, Langdon-Davies told his crowded meetings in that winter of 1940. Such plain talk could have made him as controversial (and unemployable) as Wintringham or Orwell. Langdon-Davies said it was no good blaming anybody – a policy which would help him to get on. 'It was because of a quality which I am very glad to think is possessed by almost all our countrymen. We do not like war. We hate war.'

Langdon-Davies did have left-wing political beliefs. At the end of one of his hurried little books of 1940, *Parachutes over Britain*, he evoked a slogan of the Spanish Republic – and the sense of unfinished anti-fascist business: 'The battle between right and wrong is more clearly seen now and this time they shall not pass.'

That winter lecture tour let Langdon-Davies hear what bothered his readers and listeners – so he could learn what they wanted to hear. Few writers have such a chance to understand their readership. Readers of the new experts in home defence picked up new methods, or had their ideas confirmed. Equally, any expert needed to hear from readers, to report general feelings or to pass on the best ideas, and to take up topics most asked about. The newspapers of course wanted to reflect their readers; concerns. Once the German parachutists hit the ground in the Low Countries on 10 May, home defence was the topic readers wanted to know about most – though three London papers turned down Langdon-Davies' suggestion for a page of Home Guard interests.

After his lectures Langdon-Davies 'often retired to the local pub' with Home Guard men. The talk, Langdon-Davies reported, was not of Molotov cocktails and road blocks, but civil matters; men were 'in search of this new Britain ... not something that can wait until the end of the war'.

What newspapers wanted in the summer of 1940, though, was not pub talk or Orwell's revolutionary desire for a better world, but newsworthy copy – and Langdon-Davies delivered. Even before Dunkirk had fallen, he was making sense of the threat, prophesying, and generally telling readers what to think. Under the headline 'Let us face up to reality' he warned of attempted parachute landings in the next few weeks. He wrote of a 'new technique' of invasion. First, the Fifth Column seize vital points for half an hour. Second, the advance guard arrives by parachute. Third, the main body of infantry are dropped in. Fourth, is a 'creeping barrage of bombing planes'.

Langdon-Davies' column shrank with the war years as the invasion threat receded, but by 1943 he was a major in command of a Home Guard battlecraft school. Having taken to the Home Guard so well, Langdon-Davies had put all his career eggs in one basket, which did him no good when the war was over.

CHAPTER 8

NORTHERN IRELAND

I am not your military historian. Do not turn me into an example. There are sufficient records, consult them.

Frank McGuinness, *Observe the Sons of Ulster Marching Towards the Somme*, 1985

Winston Churchill had more important things to worry about on 23 September 1940 than a memo 'remonstrance' addressed to him by Irishmen and Anglo-Irishmen wishing for Anglo-Irish peace. They protested against the Ulster Defence Volunteers being a branch of the B Special Constabulary of the Royal Ulster Constabulary (RUC), Northern Ireland's police force. Called B Specials for short, they were 'identified with all the most bitter sectarian and political differences which have long divided Northern Irish opinion'.

So what? For one thing, the signatories – including the Earl of Antrim, Major-General Gwynn and three more major-generals, and General Sir Hubert Gough – carried weight. They feared 'clashes on the Border' by forces directed by local civilians or police. Politely they suggested it all might be 'only administrative inadvertence arising from the overwhelming pressure of a stupendous conflict'. But showing they meant business, they added – on legal advice – that the arrangement was contrary to statute law. Civilian police could not take part in armed defence against an invading enemy. Defence of the realm was the responsibility of London, not the Stormont parliament in Belfast. As Churchill would have known, Hubert Gough was the man behind the Curragh Mutiny of 1914, when Army officers brought down the war minister, Churchill's then Liberal colleague Jack Seely, by 1940 Lord Mottistone. These were not men to be trifled with.

No government in London was going to fall in 1940 because of a legal mistake in Belfast, but the document did require civil servants to come up with a face-saving reply. The Home Office proposed to the Northern Ireland government at Stormont Castle that if there were any case of discrimination, Stormont should look into it. It was, it was claimed, impracticable to wind up this force of 26,000 men. Stormont wrote to the Home Office justifying its use of specials, 'In this way we were able to raise and equip in a very short space of time a body of men of proved loyalty.' In effect they were admitting they had done wrong. Stormont proposed that their LDV should cease to be special constables and should become Home Guard under the Army. But the Army pointed to 'administrative difficulties', which was a polite way of saying the Army had enough on its plate without adding age-old Irish sectarianism.

As so often, the official response was to do nothing and keep as quiet as possible. A Stormont cabinet meeting of March 1941 heard that the Imperial government had decided the Northern Ireland LDV should continue as a branch of the constabulary until taken over by the military for operational purposes; this was not to be made public until it was 'appropriate'.

Stormont had been slow to respond to the question of defence volunteers – the cabinet did not meet between 30 April and 20 May – and when it did Prime Minister Craigavon spoke of 'grave objections of which his colleagues were fully cognisant' to the establishment of a local volunteer defence corps as in Britain. 'Meanwhile B force [was] to be instructed to be prepared for any emergency,' the cabinet agreed – unpaid. Northern Ireland's ministers always had an eye on costs.

Why did Northern Ireland have to be different? A Stormont cabinet report towards a post-war history of the Home Guard pointed to the 'peculiar position' in Ireland.

> An illegal organisation [the Irish Republican Army] existed in Ireland hostile to both governments, North and South, and prepared to use force and arms against both of them. It was difficult to foresee to what extent if any attempts at espionage or sabotage would be made. Experience had shown that any serious outbreak or any successful attempts at sabotage might quickly create widespread disorder which would interfere with war production and with the training of the large number of troops in the country … which could only bring the Province into disrepute.

As the Ulster authorities justified it to themselves at the time, the B special constabulary, as a reserve to the regular police, was well placed to do the job. Each man had a service rifle and they were prepared to assist in dealing with 'any outbreak of a subversive nature'. And people did respond – 26,000 enrolled by the end of August 1940.

People in Northern Ireland seldom referred to their region's response to the threat of invasion, whether out of delicacy or because they took it for granted. There are clues. An anonymous rent collector wrote to the *Belfast Telegraph* of how in a 'certain part of the city' he saw in a kitchen a picture of Hitler and the written slogan 'Up Hitler'. The paper's editorial complained:

Volunteers are willing by the score but owing to the present unsatisfactory distribution of power, delay in organisation is unpreventable and is giving rise to
serious dissatisfaction. It is said that arms might be placed in the hands of disloyal people but the police know who are King's men and who are not.

Who was disloyal? For answers instead of cryptic words we have to turn to a
more leisurely time, after 1951, when Churchill, again Prime Minister, proposed
to form another Home Guard. The same questions came out of Belfast – use
the police as a ready-made organisation, or make a new body, as the rest of the
country did? In a 1953 exchange of letters, Lieutenant-General Jack Woodall of
Northern Ireland district headquarters at Lisburn and the new RUC Inspector-
General Captain Sir Richard Pim used different metaphors, but agreed – you
should not count the same chicken twice, and no man can serve two masters.
True, Specials were part of the civil power and strictly speaking liable to be shot
if they used arms against an invader. This was, as the men agreed, an academic
argument. Stormont, too, seemed to prefer a Home Guard, rather than a repeat of
1940. A 1951 Ministry of Home Affairs memo said there would be no question of
any political flavour attached to the Home Guard – which implied the police did
have a political flavour.

It took the Northern Ireland General Officer Commanding Lieutenant-
General R.F.S. (Reginald) Denning to call a spade a spade. He noted all B
Specials were Protestants and Unionists. And the 'reason for their existence is
to resist any attempt by Irish Nationalists to interfere by force in the affairs of
Northern Ireland particularly on the issue of Partition.' This did not put him off
using the B Specials as a kind of Home Guard already in being; he felt the danger
of invasion in World War Three was remote (and presumably Ulstermen with
rifles would not stop Soviet armies). Using specials would save money, though
the military would not influence their training.

> A secondary disadvantage is that the Home Guard under this system will inev-
> itably become as in the last war an all-Protestant organisation with political
> affiliations to the Unionist Party. RCs will not join the Home Guard under
> these circumstances.

This helps explain the August 1940 appeal by RUC Inspector-General Sir
Charles Wickham to the Ministry of Public Security for a definition of the duties
of police in an invasion. On whether to leave police in an area the enemy had
occupied, Wickham wrote:

> This is a rather more complicated question in this country. The Police here are
> and always have been armed; I do not think that this particularly affects the
> question. If an area was occupied and they were ordered to remain they would

have to hand over their arms. The difficulty is rather in the character of areas, for example South Armagh as opposed to Lisburn. On the whole I feel that we have to accept the principle that the Police should remain.

To read Wickham's code, South Armagh was a mainly Roman Catholic area; Lisburn was mainly Protestant. Anyone not Protestant might be 'disloyal', wanting to leave the Union and unite with southern Ireland. Take away the police, and sabotage, disorder, or worse (a massacre of Protestants sponsored by Germans?) might follow.

The two sides in Ireland could not sink their differences in 1940, because to do so they had to trust each other in the face of a greater enemy. Some did wish for that trust — and not only generals and earls who signed 'remonstrances'. In Workington, Alderman J.M. Cusack called on the Irish in the town to make a united demand that Craigavon and de Valera (the Dublin premier) should meet, with a view to making a united stand against the threatened invasion of Ireland.

What Alderman Cusack and most people did not know was that Craigavon had his own idea about how to make a stand in Ireland — by privately proposing to his old political friend Neville Chamberlain, no longer Prime Minister but still in the London Cabinet, an 'advance' from Northern Ireland into the south. Not surprisingly, London said no. Britain had quite enough enemies without trying to re-conquer its neutral neighbour.

CHAPTER 9

WOMEN LEFT OUT

While statesmen rally the nations, generals rally the soldiers, and soldiers heroically slaughter each other, some half the populations concerned are usually uninflamed by the battle cries. They are called women, and in the face of the epic drama of war they go on preferring dull things like gossip, small children, the price of bread, and men.

Paul Brickhill, *Escape or Die: Authentic Stories of the RAF Escaping Society*, 1952

Evelyn Jones married at the age of twenty in 1940 – her husband joined the RAF, so she lived with her family. She served with the Home Guard in Burton-on-Trent, like her father, a First World War veteran, and her younger brother, who joined aged fifteen. 'My dad volunteered me,' she recalled towards the end of her life.

> We learned, most of us learned to be what they call phonogram operators and we manned the phones, well, womanned them. And I used to go down sometimes on a Sunday morning and help the company clerk, did a bit of filing and sorting, and things like that. I used to go one or perhaps two evenings a week, I liked to go actually, I was young and foolish.

As Mrs Jones seemed to appreciate, the very language she used about her work was masculine. In Parliament, a few women MPs fought for women to enter the Home Guard, only to be mocked or fobbed off. Typical was some banter in November 1940, while Grigg was making a statement on the Home Guard in the Commons. He described the Home Guard as a 'lusty infant'. The campaigning Dr Edith Summerskill MP remarked that it was of only one sex. 'Most infants are,' Grigg replied, to the laughter of the (male majority) MPs.

Women in public life seeking more for women had long had a dilemma: did they seek equality with men, so as to do the same as men, or did they work for

The 1944 Burton Home Guard play, *According to Plan*. As the scene suggests, women played some part in home defence.

Burton Home Guards, including Evelyn Jones. Though trained to shoot by her father, she was not allowed a rifle.

better things in matters unique to women, of any class, such as childbirth? So it was with home defence. Some women demanded a rifle like 'Ready', of South Elmsall, in Yorkshire, in a letter to the press in the first week of the LDV.

> Does the Government realise that every mine village is menaced and that the women of these villages according to plan have to run into a dark corner somewhere and wait for what? Well, the women of South Elmsall have more grit than that, they are fighters every one of 'em. Hitler and his parachutists will need a lot of help afterwards – our men are working all shifts and if they are down getting coal they cannot be up above shooting Nazis for us. But we can!

If a unit did not have women, it was because the men in charge did not want any. Fred Barratt's factory had mainly women workers, but no women in the works Home Guard platoon. Fred Barratt recalled: 'I don't think he [Charlie Hodgson, the works manager and platoon commander] would have sanctioned it. Not that any [women] seemed interested.'

Women who fitted in easiest were the wives of commanders. In Hampshire, Major Wade's wife Eileen was one. In August she drove to Liphook to draw stores from battalion headquarters and delivered to the village of East Worldham 'ammunition, rations, maps, steel helmets', as Wade acknowledged in his diary.

As in any marriage, you could wonder sometimes who was giving the orders. Not far away in Winchester, Major D.C. Downes commanded A Company, later the battalion. Mrs Downes was chief clerk at company headquarters at the Guildhall, 'and her keenness and efficiency kept platoon commanders very much on the alert in their administrative work', as the unit history carefully put it.

AMAZONS

Most men – but not all – drew the line at 'Amazons'. Venetia Foster, president of the Amazons' Defence Corps, told the Hampstead branch of the Married Women's Association in July how one morning in the bath, she had thought, 'Dash it, what is going to happen to us women when the Germans come to our village?'. She was demanding that women should join the LDV on an equal footing with men, and that women in civil defence and other uniformed services should have rifle practice. 'Women in England have not yet known in their lifetime what it is to be up against it. In the pioneering days in Canada and Africa women knew how to load a gun and how to fire it.' She claimed there were 40 units of Amazons – including two at Hampstead and one at St John's Wood. They were finding it 'very difficult' to get permission to use LDV and other ranges.

On Sunday afternoon, 26 July, Dr Edith Summerskill, who lived in Highgate, watched the Hampstead unit of the Amazons at drill in a garden. An Army officer

had brought along a service rifle and gave a lecture on musketry. The unit prac-
tised drilling with walking sticks and umbrellas.

The press lapped it up. This could well be a case of a newspaper, by giving
publicity to something unusual and hence newsworthy, making a few unrepre-
sentative women look more important than they were. Less likely to make the
news were women as checkers of the ladies' toilets. Birmingham council house
had a September 1940 list of women staff suitable to 'investigate if required …
rooms reserved for ladies'.

What was women's work? It depended. Around the country in July 1940,
volunteers cleaned grease from boxed, imported rifles for the Home Guard. In
Cambridge 150 women bringing their own overalls, paraffin and rags worked for
a fortnight in the Corn Exchange to clean 6,000 rifles. Other 'women's work'
that men could pass on – much as they did in peacetime – was to do with telephones, first aid and feeding male workers. Men would do 'heavy work', such as
digging trenches and rebuilding damaged road blocks. And yet, in the crisis, some
sources seemed to suggest, normal rules would no longer apply. If food at home
ran out, people should take it from shops without paying because otherwise the
enemy would take it, according to a Reading newspaper article. Boys would have
work as messengers, 'just as [Baden Powell's] boys in the siege of Mafeking played
such a big part' in the Boer War. If traditional roles were fractured by war, would
women be able to play a different, possibly belligerent role?

> If your village is besieged there will be jobs for everyone, but whatever the job,
> there is a motto for man, woman, boy and girl. It is this; don't give in. don't lose
> your head. Don't panic.

At the 'demob' of the organisation in 1944 the official total of Home Guards
was 1,727,095 compared with 30,696 women auxiliaries, as permitted from April
1943. So even then, a battalion of several hundred Home Guards might have only
a dozen women. In 1940, some defence units did have women, on the quiet.
There is evidence that men wrote women's work out of the record. Lady Rachel
Egerton, the East Sussex county WVS (Women's Voluntary Service) organiser,
sent a draft report on her women's work on civil defence in 1940 to the county
council clerk, H.S. Martin. In February 1941 Martin wrote back, suggesting that
Lady Rachel take out a mention of women filling Molotov cocktails, 'as I think
such activities are really outside the scope of your organisation'. Lady Egerton
replied at once that she felt the report should include it, but Martin must have got
his way; the copy on file has nothing about ladies' cocktails.

Judging by the records of the Inspectorate of Home Guard, which was meeting more than once a week in mid-1940 under Pownall, the Army neither went
out of its way to draw in women, nor did it try to root out local recruitment of
females, having more pressing things to do. The Inspectorate's ninth meeting on

19 July heard of 'typists urgently needed'. It was proposed to allow ten per cent of enrolled personnel to be women – which in a million-man body would have meant 100,000. A Colonel Archdale said they were 'trying to kill this question', but a Colonel Sir E.G. Warner said there was a demand for female clerical assistance; 'they [women] were already doing a lot of voluntary work'. Three meetings later, on 31 July, a memo had gone to the Prime Minister, but Warner pointed out (again) that women were 'already functioning'. On 9 August the issue came up yet again: 'WVS were prepared to play and the policy really is are they wanted.' The 16 August meeting heard that entry of women was in the hands of the Secretary of State for War. In other words, the military awaited a political decision. At the next meeting on 20 August, the question was put to bed, 'postponed until autumn'. Whether women ought to be in the Home Guard never cropped up in Pownall's diary, which suggests he had bigger things to grumble about.

Women of course had a say about what men did inside the family home; though to what degree is anyone's guess. Fred Barratt consulted his wife before he set off to the police station on the night of the Eden broadcast. How many wives told their husbands not to go? Of those men, how many gave in? Captain E.A.G. Marlar, Lichfield Home Guard leader, warning of falling numbers of Home Guards in 1941, appealed to wives and mothers, because 'their influence upon the Home Guard is considerable'. 'Good men have been lost to us because wives do not like being left at home alone in the evenings. This is only natural.' A man would never let on to another – except in jest – that his wife wore the trousers. Alternatively, would a man who did not want to risk his neck, or even simply make any effort, blame his wife for keeping him at home?

A Bristol Home Guard company's newsletter in 1943 praised the ladies of 1940 for taking in and adjusting their husbands' first uniforms. Men's pride was jolted when they came home the first time with rifle and bayonet:

> To be sternly told for heaven's sake put that horrible thing away, and don't let the children see it. What you didn't know of course is that our greatest pride that day was to display to you all that newly acquired piece of armament. Still, we grinned and did as we were told.

CHAPTER 10

SPIES, SABOTEURS AND THE FIFTH COLUMN

There is only one topic of conversation these days; Fifth Column.
Berwick Advertiser, 23 May 1940

On the last day of peace, 2 September 1939, police special constables were putting on their steel helmets like Howard Channon, the chief reporter of the *Derby Evening Telegraph*. In an article typed that month, filed for use after the war and only printed 50 years later, Channon wrote: 'The same night I did my first guard duty on the Corporation waterworks at Little Eaton which, like all other vulnerable points in the county were patrolled throughout the night (we still had the IRA scare if you remember).'

Handily near the Home Guard headquarters of 19 Platoon (Long Wittenham) in Oxfordshire, was The Plough pub. Corporal Chambers was the landlord. The village's Home Guards could be ready for duty, and in the pub, at the same time. One night in the winter of 1940, the telephone rang and Chambers answered. 'Conversation suddenly ceased and one dart player even paused, hand raised ready.' A lady was reporting that she had seen lights and was sure it was fifth columnists. What happened in that year to make the British assume that a light in the dark was a fifth columnist – and not, as it almost invariably turned out to be, a farmer or motorist?

After the shock of the 10 May parachute landings in the Low Countries, British civilians were struggling to make sense of the Germans' success. At times it seemed as if the British would believe in any Nazi trickery rather than credit the Germans with out-thinking and out-fighting them. Civilians filled the gaps with tales. One newspaper diarist repeated the story of two nuns, parachutists in disguise, caught on a train, a 'fairytale' he compared with the First World War story of trains of Russian soldiers spotted with snow on their boots, heading for the coast and the trenches. (That particular rumour was, if not actively encouraged, certainly not denied by the British. See the book *Conceal, Create, Confuse* by Martin Davies.)

Above left: An aerial view of Scarborough harbour.

Above right: South Bay in Scarborough. In 1914, the town was one of the areas of the north-east coast shelled by German warships.

The British authorities did not have much to go on. A 22 May general order, forwarded to all police, gave a colourful picture of German parachutists in the Netherlands. Supposedly parachutists disguised themselves as Dutch, French and British soldiers, and also as civilians, such as priests, peasants and schoolboys. Young boys dressed as girls, girls dressed as nurses, and servant girls landed where they had worked as domestic servants, it was claimed.

Those dressed as girls (that is, men and women) carried baskets full of hand grenades made to look like provisions. Automatic rifles were hidden under female clothing. Some carried poisoned cigarettes and chocolates. 'Included were a number of Poles who had no idea where they had landed or what they were to do other than to shoot anything they saw.' One unconfirmed source, a captured parachutist, reckoned that IRA members would be parachuted in when England's turn came.

Even hysterical stories were impossible to disprove. Once newspapers aired the most absurd stories, they were taken as gospel. At a meeting of commanders in chief under Ironside on 2 June, one agenda item was the danger caused by press stories of Germans landing 'dressed as nuns, parsons, officers etc'. According to the minutes, 'Stories are likely to decrease as troops and the general public become used to the present conditions.' So the authorities had no answer to the stories, except to let them die out.

At least one newspaper fell for German propaganda. The Isle of Wight weekly reported William Joyce, 'Lord Haw Haw', the English traitor broadcasting from Germany, saying that he would like to holiday again at Freshwater Bay, after the war. He supposedly gave news about the island. The paper suggested the only way he knew was by secret wireless transmitter; 'evidently there are traitors in our midst'. The next week, the newspaper admitted the news was hearsay and nobody had actually heard the broadcasts. 'Previous stories of this kind have been submitted by the authorities to our intelligence service who take records of all the German wireless broadcasts and in every case they have proved groundless.'

Newspapers wanted it all ways, printing an official denial and so putting the original story in print. The Stratford on Avon weekly had the headline 'Mayor denies ridiculous rumour that he is a German.' The mayor had close cropped hair; to some people, that made him look like a German. It was ridiculous, but not ridiculous enough to leave out of the paper.

LOOSE TALK

As some did point out at the time, the risk of real fifth columnists – enemy agents, whether fascists or communists, passing radio messages to Germany, or ready to rise up when the invader came – was small. Rumours abounded, which, so some believed, did the Germans' work by spreading gloom. Gossip could eat away at one man's trust in another. Parliament responded; 'making a statement likely to cause alarm' became an offence.

Significantly, when such cases of defeatist talk did reach the courts, usually the police themselves had happened to be listening. This suggests that most people regarded talk as just that, and not worth going to the police about. To take a July case, reprinted widely in the press, a detective was in the smoke of the Queens Hotel in Ashby in Leicestershire, when he heard three farmers discussing the war. One of them, Hubert Bourne, said: 'They will beat us easily. They have taken all the countries they wanted so far and a small country like this can't stop them coming here.' Though as he told the court, 'it is my opinion,' the fine was 25 guineas.

In August, a garage hand was in court in Liverpool for causing a public mischief. Signing himself 'A Britisher', he had written to the city's chief constable on 5 July claiming he knew of 'a fifth column agency'. Two women with German money and Nazi sympathies knew what jobs were in dock, so he claimed. A detective found the letter-writer, who admitted: 'I let my imagination run riot.' Why? Was he mentally unbalanced? Did he want to make a stir? Did he have something against the women? It was not for the court to ask.

Some cases were even odder, like the 50-year-old German arrested trying to get into conversation with soldiers in Regent Street in London. He was wearing women's silk stockings and high heeled shoes. There was no suggestion the man was a spy, though police at first suspected so. A woman gave evidence that the refugee dressed the same way in Germany. While newspaper reports gave no hint, the man was no fifth-columnist but presumably batted for the other side. He was jailed for six months.

The problem was 'too much indiscreet talk', to quote a Sheffield newspaperman's story of going home on a bus. He sat in front of a man on defence work, who boasted to a lady that he was patrolling on the outskirts of the city for a vital purpose, 'which he mentioned in tone loud enough for me to hear quite clearly'.

Pillbox on the Trent and Mersey Canal.

Like most crimes, the cases that reached court or the papers were only a fraction of the whole. How many more loud-mouths or gloomy people were there, and how defeatist were the defeatists – was it only talk, or action? It's one of many unknowns of 1940. There are enough hints in the papers of defeatism once France was falling. Lewes MP Rear-Admiral T.P.H. Beamish told his Conservative association: 'You will meet people who will say they [Germans] are invincible, let them come and let us have peace.'

The defeatists – or realists who were only speaking their mind – courted anonymity. Too little trust could be as harmful as too much, if people became so suspicious that they would not take orders from anyone. General Ironside in his Chester speech deplored that the British were a 'most unsuspicious people', but appealed for a happy medium: 'We do not want a spy complex but neither do we want any fifth column trouble.'

Fears were affecting the ability of people to identify the obvious. In June the Hofor (Home forces) teleprinter sent a message to the regions about 'cryptic signs' in chalk and paint on telegraph poles. The Army told all volunteers to watch for persons marking telegraph poles. The markings – others were spotted on pavements – were by post office engineers, or council workmen, as was usual in peacetime.

WORRIED SIR WILFRID

Even senior people felt unnerved by the sudden Nazi victories. Sir Wilfrid Greene, as was only fitting for the Master of the Rolls, took his worries to the very top. He said he had some very alarming information that he wanted to impart to the Prime Minister alone. Churchill delegated the matter to his gate-keeper, General Ismay, noting that the Master of the Rolls had no right to ask for the PM alone. Churchill did ask for a report, though, and so on 6 June, Ismay wrote to Churchill that he had had an hour's talk with Sir Wilfrid.

> The burden of his song was that of foreseen parachutists and fifth column. He harped on the intimate knowledge of this country which had been acquired by an immense number of Nazi youth in the course of their Strength from Joy tours of this country and quoted a number of incidents of which he himself had been a witness before the war – he felt that the imminence of the danger was not realised and that our defensive preparations were inadequate for the scale of possibilities … He had nothing to say we have not heard before – in fact to be perfectly frank he gave me the impression of a man who is labouring under an obsession … [Greene] having got it off his chest would desist from troubling you any further.

Churchill's response was 'Gen Ismay you may well let him read my memo of four years ago, parachute and airborne landings, to show him that there is nothing novel in this WSC 17/6.'

ROAD KILL

A number of innocent motorists were killed by guards at road blocks, because the men were nervy or too quick to shoot. The trouble stemmed from guns in the hands of untrained men and boys. Some could see trouble coming. The headmaster of Charterhouse, Robert Birley, wrote to Southern Command on 28 May, as the private school at Godalming in Surrey was within the Southern Command area. (Presumably not wanting to be a troublemaker, Birley did add that he was writing at the suggestion of Sir George Schuster, vice-chairman of the governing body, someone we have already met.) About 120 boys and 20 masters, he reported, had joined an LDV section. They were responsible for the school grounds, 'which are of course extensive'. Birley asked for 'any information you can give us about our activities. It is very important that we should know what is really expected of Public Schoolboys.' He assumed that the main duty was to observe and report quickly and accurately. He came to the point: the local, outside commander had instructed all LDVs on duty that if they challenged twice and had no reply, they should fire. 'I am more than doubtful whether this is even legal and I cannot possibly allow these instructions to be given to boys before I am satisfied on this point.'

As early as 7 June, because some of its officers had to travel by night, Aldershot command urged military and LDV posts to use their 'common sense'. Those two words cropped up often in 1940, as if everyone would know what to do as a result.

On 24 June Edward Bainbridge, Gateshead chief constable, passed on a civil defence complaint to Major E.H. Kirkup, the LDV commander in Gateshead, about three LDV men firing rifles in the night. Civil defence people claimed to be 'definitely scared to move about during air raid warnings'. A similar letter, dated 12 June, went up the chain of command from an anti-aircraft officer based at RAF Hucknall. He reported one of his officers wounded in a car. Twice in three nights he was challenged on the open road, once by guards without any light. The guards could have been parachutists trying to steal a car, the officer wrote, and he would have felt justified in shooting. He called for properly organised and equipped road blocks. A Brigadier Kay of Northern Command at York passed on the letter and ordered the 'folly' of untrained sentries to stop. Gradually the message trickled down to the guards on the roads, though shootings went on all summer.

Absurdly, in an invasion, road blocks would delay the very mobile columns that were the country's best hope against invaders. Three Australian battalions carried by civilian motor coaches were to destroy any airborne troops landing on Salisbury Plain. A conference in July saw 'difficulty … in passing column through road blocks manned by LDVs'. The troops had two methods: sound the horn and flash headlights, or send a dispatch rider ahead – all in the hope that nervous guards would not shoot first. No wonder the conference added that 'alternative methods are being investigated'.

RADIO LISTENERS

A police file now in the Bristol record office gives an insight into the national effort to capture agents sending radio messages. The security services were searching even before the war. MI5 had sent circulars to police in July and September 1939 about detecting illicit wireless transmissions, asking: 'It is of the greatest importance that the police should refrain from taking precipitate direct action in these matters.' In April 1940, an Adrian Simpson for Major-General Sir Vernon Kell of the security service, whose address was a London box number, wrote that its radio security section (RSS, known also as MI8) accepted four Bristol voluntary interceptors, living in Fishponds, Henleaze, Westbury on Trym and Clifton. Earlier the city's Chief Constable Charles Maby had sent names of people considered suitable for 'employment upon special wireless listening duties'.

By June 1940 a memo to police from the Home Office explained that RSS regional officers, all captains, were in Exeter, Cardiff, Leicester, Preston, Stirling,

York, Cambridge and London. The voluntary civilian interceptors would supplement any listening by police or others. The interceptors would listen for any transmissions about the weather – presumably of use to the Luftwaffe – the war, or British fascists or communists. If finds were urgent, the interceptors could ring a couple of London numbers; otherwise, they should write to the security services.

In August 1940, the Exeter branch of RSS sent Maby a list of 22 voluntary interceptors in Bristol. If that ratio was similar around the country, it suggests a national total of 700 such individuals. A Brigadier Harker of the security service wrote to police in August 1940 about suspected radio transmissions. As he said, the public was telling police of suspicious wireless transmissions. Harker gave the wavelengths and a short description of the three German radio stations aimed at England. The 'New British Broadcasting Station' (NBBS) claimed to be a pirate station on behalf of the man in the street. It usually ended its day with 'God Save the King'. Workers Challenge was 'virulently Communist, defeatist, using obscene language, the speaker having a spurious Cockney accent'. And Radio Caledonia was an alleged Scottish national station. Harker considered that morale was unlikely to be much harmed. The NBBS show was 'somewhat dull and uninspiring', while Workers Challenge was 'of such excessive vulgarity'. It was however 'being carefully monitored'. As for rumours that Lord Haw Haw gave details of local events such as troop movements, hundreds of stories had been checked, Harker said. Almost without exception, the German announcer did not refer to a local incident. In other words, the stories were 'wilfully spread by some underground organisation either mischievous or definitely inspired by enemy agents with a view to impressing the British public with the omniscience of the German intelligence services'. This, Harker said, could do harm and cause alarm. He added that in the last few days a fourth enemy propaganda station, New Christian Peace Movement, had begun. It was ending with the hymn 'O God our help in Ages Past', and put out 'biblical matter in a blasphemous format'.

Acting on what the civilian and military radio-interceptors found were dozens of security service vans with mobile direction finding apparatus based around Britain and Northern Ireland.

ROUND-UP

In an invasion, police had about 1,000 male and female suspects to arrest nationally – British and foreign – under defence regulations. The Home Office sent a list to chief constables in May 1941, replacing one from August 1940. The form of words would be that because of recent conduct or writing or speaking recently, police believed the person likely to assist the enemy. Police would give those arrested enough time to pack a bag or suitcase, but not more. Women would go to eight prisons, men to 30 'collecting centres', usually barracks. Within 48 hours the prisoners would go by train to Longsight in Manchester, then to a transit camp at nearby Belle Vue. The Home Office defined the suspects not as criminals awaiting trial, but persons believed to be ready if given the opportunity to act in a manner dangerous to the state. 'They are to be treated with as much consideration as circumstances permit but they must be guarded with the greatest vigilance as some might make determined attempts to escape.' Who the individuals were is unclear.

PARACHUTES

Enough unexplained things happened all summer to keep people guessing. George Lane, the Kidderminster watch repairer, wrote in his diary in September: 'I forgot to mention that on 14 August empty parachutes were dropped on this town in several places, the nearest being in the cemetery about 100 yards from the bedroom window which we were looking through at 8am in time to see police folding it up.'

The Home Office wrote to chief constables on 17 August about three separate findings of parachutes dropped on the night of 13/14 August, and a package of maps and papers 'including some clumsily faked instructions purporting to be directed to saboteurs landed in the country'. Civilians were not to know the drops were meant to confuse.

A dozen empty parachutes turned up on the border of Staffordshire and Derbyshire, which prompted a military search. Ralph Besant of the village of Sudbury was on summer holiday as a county scholarship boy at Ashbourne Grammar School. He recalled the request of a Sudbury estate worker, Richard 'Gassy' Taylor.

> When the parachutes came overnight he collected me – I lived very near to this [disused] gas works – and he took me over to the gas works – under one of the chimneys it's a very dark chamber, probably where they cleaned the flues; as children we used to play in them, but rather frightening; and he said, would you go in there and see if there is a German. I declined.

A CATCH

Despite the overreactions, the cranks, and the people who could not resist passing on gossip, in the village of Denton outside Northampton, the Home Guard made a genuine catch. On the afternoon of 2 September a man was spotted in a ditch in a field, with a suitcase. When challenged to produce his identity card, the stranger showed a Birmingham address, but written in continental style, with the street name first and then the number, and a wrong date. The huge knot in his tie was suspiciously 'un-English'. Even more un-English, the man carried an automatic pistol and a wallet containing £300. He admitted his suitcase (holding a portable radio transmitter) had cracked him on the head when landing. Police took him away.

At 4am on 3 September, four men landed in a rowing boat between Dymchurch and Hythe. Three were arrested, and police sent warnings to other forces around the country before the fourth was caught. The four admitted they were enemy aliens, sent to gain information about coastal defences and British morale. They were supposed to travel by night and hide by day and make their way to a port to embark for abroad. According to the prisoners, others were trained for the work and expected to come to Britain.

CHAPTER 11

SEPTEMBER 1940: THE GENERAL TALKS BOLLOCKS

It has been apparent that the longer Hitler looks at the prospect of a struggle with the British Empire the less he likes it. While we have no wish to lull ourselves into a feeling of false security by exaggerating the defensive value of being an island … our insularity is from this point of view our strength.
Burton Daily Mail editorial, 22 July 1940

By September, time was running out for the feared German onslaught; the nights were drawing in and the weather would become too changeable to make an invasion by sea or air practical. Pownall was still touring the country in between inspectorate meetings in London, making him a well-qualified judge. His views on invasion varied. In his diary for 19 August he wrote: 'I can't imagine that Hitler will attempt invasion until he has got our air force brought near down and out.' On 17 September, after a week in the west of England from Cumberland to Camarthen, he was admitting to himself

At first I thought it was something of a bluff, again part of the war of nerves. But he has now collected so much in the way of ships and barges along the western seaboard of Holland, Belgium and France that it really looks as if he means business. … I don't see how he could hope to bring off a successful invasion whilst we have an air force in being and he has failed to put our air force out of business … I can't imagine that his military advisers like the idea. But he has overruled them many times and got away with it.

Saturday 7 September had seen the signal word 'Cromwell' go out, for a national mobilising of Home Guards, not that Churchill or the newspapers remarked on it. That was not the same as saying the Germans were sailing, though for at least some Home Guards, it felt like the time had come. When some Home Guards

Field Marshal Montgomery as CIGS (Chief of Imperial General Staff) designate in the Viceregal Gardens, New Delhi in 1946 with the Viceroy, Field Marshal Wavell and Commander-in-Chief of the Indian Army, Field Marshal Sir Claude Auchinleck. In 1940 Monty was the most junior of the three; by 1946 he was the most senior and famous.

had assembled on the outskirts of Luton, the battalion commander put his head in the doorway and said: 'Gentlemen; I have grave news for you; it has begun.' In the sky was a red glow, presumably from the bombing of London and anti-aircraft searchlights.

Auchinleck at Southern Command in Salisbury sent a special order of the day on 20 September that meant enough to the commander of a Home Guard battalion on the outskirts of Oxford to quote in print after the war. Auchinleck wrote of how the enemy was said to be ready to invade. Men must not be surprised, and must be on their toes at all times.

> We must at all times be ready to defend every post and every position from attack from any direction and must always be on the watch against attack from the flanks or rear ... Forewarned is forearmed and no trick or ruse will avail the enemy if we remember that there are only two orders which really matter and from which nothing should distract us. For those in front line positions 'hang on'; for those in reserve, 'push on'.

Auckinleck posted a copy on 22 September from his headquarters with a chatty letter to Ismay – 'my dear Pug' – and signed 'Claude'.

> Opinion seems to be divided amongst the powers that be as to the true value of the information we received last night. I was at Plymouth staying with the naval c in c who woke me at 5am to tell me the news. However we are taking no chances. The enclosed may amuse you!!! Grandiloquent bollocks?!!

Montgomery had taken over from Auchinleck at 5 Corps on 22 July – everyone rising in rank to fill the gap made by Brooke's rise to the top. Montgomery was not the kind of man to write 'grandiloquent bollocks'. For the professional,

September was a long month of uncertainty. The 5 Corps intelligence summary for the week 7–13 September said that 'In general though all available information goes to show that an invasion is in fact intended, there has been no definite indication that the final decision has been reached.' Meanwhile a tactical summary spoke of a 'heightened imminence of invasion', because of 'massing of German sea transport in Channel ... Whether invasion was intended and was broken up by RAF attacks on Channel ports or whether merely the threat was intended had not become clear by the end of the month.'

In Leamington Spa, A.J. Brown was the man in his Home Guard platoon responsible for calling out his fellows in an emergency. They gathered at the town's drill hall.

> I remember the night or rather early Sunday morning about 1am early in September 1940 when I was awakened by the urgent ringing of the doorbell. My section sergeant was at the door and said, 'Home Guard call-out'. In about ten minutes I was out on my cycle doing the same to the men on my list. It operated very effectively and in about half an hour all were ready for action. Some of the platoons had been issued with denim uniforms but my platoon (number four) was still using the LDV arm band. On arriving at the Drill Hall I joined the queue at the armoury where rifles and ammunition were being issued by a regular Army sergeant. When my turn came he hesitated. I must have been his first customer in civilian clothes for he said, 'They will shoot you as a franc tireur'. I replied that 'they will shoot me in any case, if they get the chance, so let us have some ammo.' I received a rifle and a bandolier of ammunition. When my platoon was complete we marched to the corner of Archery Road by the bowling greens. Other platoons were on other corners nearby.

There they stayed until an 'all clear' message at 8am.

The same night – 7/8 September 1940 – the order came to D Company on Cannock Chase to man all road blocks.

> It was pitch black and raining hard at the time, and as no preliminary warning or rumours had been heard, it was felt that as this was no time for a joke the situation must be really serious, with the enemy actually landed, or about to land, any minute. The road blocks had been sited some time before and some material had been got together for the purpose of impeding enemy traffic, but no previous practice at night had been carried out in the manning of these blocks. All platoons turned out well, live ammunition was fetched in a hand-cart from Chasetown Police Station, where it was stored at that time, and amidst subdued excitement five rounds were handed to each man to be loaded in the magazine, bolt closed over, the safety catches on. This was the first time many of the men had carried live ammunition, and as they marched off from company HQ

to their respective road blocks the company commander waited with outward unconcern, but with inward trepidation for the sound of the opening shot, not being able to feel at all sure whether the first victim would be an innocent civilian, a policeman, or a genuine Hun. However, nothing untoward happened, and by 2pm the next day the worst of the scare was over.

Farmer's son Wilf Hodgson was an original LDV in the Coningsby and Tattershall unit in Lincolnshire. On this Saturday night, at about midnight his unit had to report to headquarters – Coningsby village hall – for weapons, ammunition and orders – to man all observation checkpoints. His task was to check traffic on the main street.

> Now, a lot of people took exception at the best of times to being stopped by the Home Guard and ordered to produce identification and at this particular time, a regiment of Gordon Highlanders was stationed in the village. You can imagine the state some of them were in after a night in the local pub drinking their national tipple. Let's just say they were not best pleased to see us!

He did not question why he was on guard in case of invasion, and regular soldiers were not.

OPENED LETTERS

People did seem in good heart, judging by the report to the Cabinet on 30 August titled 'Home opinion as shewn in mails to USA and Eire'. The authorities read people's mail to friends and family abroad, seeking to understand public opinion on many topics, besides invasion. As for writers to America,

> … fear of invasion is almost nil … opinion is fairly equally divided as to whether it will be attempted or not. Those who think it will not come base their argument on our complete preparedness to meet it; those who expect it consider for the same reason that it is doomed to failure. Among the former are a number of writers who openly fear that it will not be attempted.

The report dealt separately with mail to Eire, because 'writers in this mail are on the whole of a lower social grade than those of the American mail but the standard of morale is equally high and confidence in the ultimate victory is general.' Opinion was again divided as to whether Hitler would attempt invasion or not.

Could you believe what people wrote in private letters? Not necessarily. Mrs Henry Daubeney the elderly novelist in Lewes, whose daughter lived in the United States, admitted fear of invasion to her diary, but even before the war in letters to her daughter she avoided touching on any kind of bad news, such as her daughter's and her own money worries.

A PLAN IN A GARAGE

Were the Germans coming? And if so, where? What the Germans intended, what the British authorities thought, and what both sides speculated in public, were three separate things. Years later, advancing Allied soldiers found a garage on the outskirts of Brussels full of maps prepared by the German Army for the invasion of Britain and Ireland; hundreds of thousands of dossiers; and green envelopes, their contents including reproductions of street maps and aerial photographs. The general plan of the German campaign became public for the first time. *The Times* reported on 18 October 1944:

> The first phase of the invasion after the battle for air supremacy had been won apparently included attempts to sink blockships at the entrance to the principal east coast estuaries and harbours with the intention of impeding the deployment of our naval forces. Then it would seem as far as England was concerned that there were to have been two main landings in the south with airborne landings in the Midlands and behind the east coast. The first of the southern attacks was to have been in Kent and Sussex; the object of the Kentish attack was to get into the Weald and thus to turn the line of the south downs; but the general purpose of this whole landing was to attract what field army Britain possessed at the time to the defence of London against an attack coming from the south.
>
> Then it would appear that the second attack was to be put in, a landing in the neighbourhood of Portland and Weymouth with the intention of getting the

Two views of Mullion Cove on the south Cornish coast between Penzance and Falmouth. In November 1940, a paper on the UK's military defence reckoned that the south-west, excluding the north coast of Devon and Cornwall, had 378 miles of coastline, of which 118 were suitable for armoured vehicles to land.

armour into the admirable tank country which stretches from the borders of Devon up to Salisbury Plain and the Cotswolds.

From this position the best way into London was according to the German notes south-eastward through Bicester so that while the British field army was fighting on the North Downs facing south, London would be taken in the rear by the armoured forces. Apparently also the Germans envisaged that the final stage of the invasion of England would be a last ditch stand by the remnants of the British forces pushed back into North Wales.

As we know, the German air force never won the necessary air supremacy so that the Germany navy and army could do as it pleased.

A BRIEF BURST OF STORIES

The end of the war saw a flurry of tales about the 1940 invasion that never was deemed newsworthy by the press. More documents in Germany confirmed the information in the garage papers about the planned invasion. The first interviews with captured generals began to explain why the Germans had not invaded when they had the chance. For one thing, they had lacked the right boats. In Norway, at the trial of the traitor Quisling, a leading Nazi told the court that he and his friends were so sure that Germany would conquer Britain that they discussed how long the air trip from Norway to Britain would take and where they should take houses in Britain.

Speaking in Parliament in May 1945, Churchill remembered

> … how in the first months of this administration the King would come in from practising with his rifle and tommy gun in his garden of Buckingham Palace. If it had come to a last stand in London, a matter which all had to consider at some time, I have no doubt his Majesty would have come very near to departing from his constitutional rectitude by disregarding the advice of his ministers.

He was hinting that King George VI, a First World War naval veteran after all, would have perished in a 'last stand' in his capital. Presumably, the Queen and the two Princesses would have gone overseas as fight-on figureheads, like the Dutch and Norwegian monarchs. Although when it had been suggested that the Princesses Margaret and Elizabeth be evacuated to Canada, the Queen replied, 'The children won't go without me. I won't leave the King. And the King will never leave.'

In the general election campaign of June 1945, Churchill touched on 1940.

> What did we do? All over the world people expected us to give in but not in England. There was no thought of giving in. I have often been praised for the

Carbis Bay. Though on the north tip of Cornwall and well away from anywhere strategic, the defenders had no way of knowing for sure that the Germans would not land here.

part taken at that moment but nothing could be easier. All I did was to express the heartfelt feeling and the resolve of the British people that we would see the war through.

Though commendably modest, Churchill was telling people what they wanted to hear, rather than the messy truth of 1940. The people voted him out in any case.

These stories of what might have been gradually petered out. People flocked to the seaside in the summer of 1945, although the remnants of defences from 1940 made it a risky business. It had taken more than 18 months' work – and the deaths of more than 100 men – to remove thousands of mines, exploded by high pressure water jets, or uncovered by armoured bulldozers and mine detectors.

A FINAL RUMOUR

One of the many strange beliefs of 1940, explained in the press in 1945 as something spread by 'British intelligence', casts doubt on how well-informed people were – or wanted to be. A story persisted that the Germans did invade, but were bloodily thrown out, or burned at sea and washed up. George Lane confided to his diary on 17 September 'There is a rumour about that they have already tried a landing and been repulsed but no news officially.'

The number of supposed dead Germans ranged from tens to thousands, even hundreds of thousands. A queer detail was that the Germans supposedly advertised that they would pay a reward of the equivalent of three shillings for each dead, clothed German soldier. The story found legs in late 1944 from the newly-liberated Belgians.

Where were the dozens, hundreds, of British airmen who fired on the invasion fleet, or the men who set fire to the sea, to burn the Germans in oil – let alone the men who handled the dead bodies? Was such astonishing news not the talk of airfields, pubs, and the whole country? Newspaper articles got around that, by claiming that Britain never 'openly' admitted invasion. Yet surely it would have been in Britain's interests to hail a victory, and give out a medal. It never happened.

POWNALL'S VERDICT

Pownall summed up in his diary on 29 September. He was about to leave the Home Guard for a command in Northern Ireland. 'The Home Guard are indeed a peculiar race. There are so many "ins and outs", so much local prejudice and so many conflicting currents and opinion within it.' He claimed civilians lacked sympathy with the Home Guard, only to show remarkably little sympathy himself, calling them 'a troublesome and querulous lot, the Home Guard. There is mighty little pleasing them and the minority is always noisy.'

At least Pownall had travelled around the country and could claim to have seen it for himself. Much of the friction over the 'invasion summer' stemmed from the collision of two ways of working, military and civilian, which in peacetime seldom met. The military (and civilians who took their side) gave and obeyed

The 1904 plaque between Clacton and Frinton-on-Sea marking a military exercise – a landing – attended by royalty, shows that the fear of an invasion dated from before the First World War.

Two Home Guard men with Tommy gun and Bren
light machine-gun, Dorking, Surrey. (War Office
official photograph by Len Puttnam, 1 December 1940)

orders. The civilian had the right to answer
back, to play politics, to take a tea-break,
to claim a problem was not theirs. Home
Guards were volunteers, civilian part-timers
in uniform, neither one nor the other.

Other bugbears of the Home Guard
played themselves out over the next four
years. If higher identified problems and
offered solutions to all local commanders,
might some local men resent being told
what to do? Who should have the last say,
the local commander or the central authority? The volunteer 'spirit' would disappear if
the Home Guard had proper officer ranks
and serving became compulsory, as it did
by 1942. But how else could command-
ers impose discipline to ensure the simplest thing, men turning up? At Corby
steel works on 23 September 1940 Captain Woolley told the Home Guard ranks
'There can be no place for the half-hearted shirker or shrimshanker who must be
weeded out of the battalion without delay.' At a parade a month before, 35 men
attended and 28 did not. This was 'disgraceful … no adequate defence can be
based on a system permitting this gross breach of duty by men who have undertaken serious military obligations in the defence of their country.'

How was Britain to get its people to work harder than they would in peacetime, to deter or defeat an invasion? Most people would only realise what they
had lost too late, when the swastika was flying from their town hall. Might some
not mind, even then?

Such uncomfortable questions went to the heart of how hard Britain wanted
to fight, and what sort of nation it was, war or not. To recall Auchinleck's cynical
private letter to Ismay, were all the stirring calls by leaders to their men, to fight,
merely patronising 'bollocks'? We can say that Auchinleck's letter shows he felt
comfortable ('my dear Pug') and confident that his attitude would be understood
by a fellow general. Even when the need for all to pull together was never plainer,
was something phoney going on?

CHAPTER 12

CONCLUSION

One might think that there is nothing new to add. At least, one is tempted to think that way until one starts to examine what actually is said and what is not said.
Norman Davies, *No Simple Victory; Europe at War, 1939–1945,* 2007

'To become a skilled pianist needs years of training but most of us can learn to play one single tune and that is what is needed.' That might be the epitaph for the Home Guard and everyone who scrambled to defend their country from May 1940. The writer was our old friend Sir George Schuster MP, as sure of himself as ever in two long articles on the Home Guard in *The Times* in October 1940. Schuster began with complaints about of lack of direction and confusion in the chain of command; delay in equipment; and the proliferation of 'paper'. '[These] must not be allowed to obscure the greatness of the total achievement for which of course the main credit is due to the volunteers themselves.'

For the volunteers in one village, Binsted in Hampshire, the year ended unhappily. The watch from the church tower ended on 1 October because of the cold. H.V. Morton, the commander, scribbled in the log book

On the night of the eighth [November 1940] I went at 9.30pm to inspect the guard. I discovered the guard room empty, the stove burning, the light on, govt property lying about.

He saw one of the men in uniform at a whist drive.

I saw no sign of the patrol although I waited an hour. I am not prepared to say whether they were doing their duty or sitting in a friend's cottage. With an NCO i/c who attends a whist drive anything is possible. They may even have been in bed although that is not likely because their bicycles were in the guardroom.

Pillbox at Scropton on the River Dove.

Pillbox covering the River Trent at Burton-on-Trent.

In the morning, Morton rang the NCO and asked for his resignation. Morton suspended the Binsted section, and listed the men's excuses – mainly 'working with cattle'. You wonder if Morton appreciated quite how long and hard a cattle-man had to work; if an empty guard room was such a crime, even in 1940; and if a better commander than Morton might have had a quiet word with his men, or given them training, so that they did not think to play whist. For a professional writer, Morton never came across as a man who saw two sides to a story.

WHO WERE THE HOME GUARDS?

In moments of crisis it never occurs to anybody to ask the ordinary people what they are thinking.
John Scanlon, *But Who Has Won?* (1939)

'The spirit of 1914 is still alive in the breasts of many fathers,' shown by the rush of volunteers, claimed a village correspondent of the *Warrington Guardian* in the May launch week of the LDV. Few if any others spoke of the 'spirit of 1914' in 1940. A minority of people had adult memories of that year. Perhaps the year was best forgotten; too many people had gone to war and come back wounded in mind or body, or not come back at all. But the correspondent had a point. The men of 1940 volunteered for the same reasons as in 1914. They laid aside family and career out of a sense of duty or for love of country; because it made a change; or because their friends, neighbours and workmates did. 'We're here because we're here', they sang.

Thanks to the mid-war parish invasion committee of Carleton Rode, near Norwich, we have a list of the village Home Guard men, their ages and addresses. Their lieutenant and commander was H.W. (Harry) Cook, aged 57, who ran a motor car garage. His second in command, Sergeant Brook, 40, like six other volunteers, lived in the village's row of council houses. Corporals Jay and Wright were aged 28 and 25. The lance-corporals were Bowley, aged 36; Dick Newman, aged 41; and John Tye, a 32-year-old farmer. The ages of the 48 privates ranged from 18 to 65. So a fair chunk of the village men – according to the last census in 1931, the village had 578 people – were in the Home Guard. Did that make them representative of the nation?

Some were men of 1914–18. Others were young and keen. Douglas Young in Hampshire was one of them.

A lot of chaps were in the Home Guard really because they felt it was the thing to do, but they had no ambitions to do anything, but me, at my age, I was a bit enthusiastic, and I was desperate to get in the forces and I just grabbed at every opportunity.

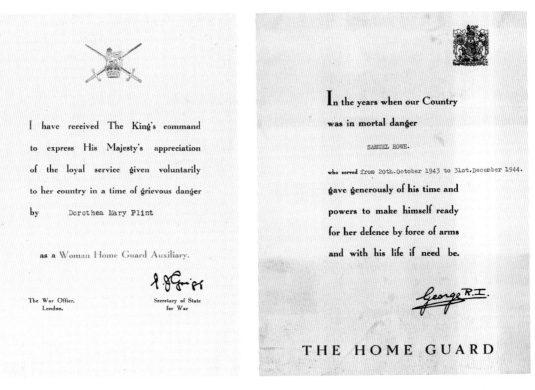

I have received The King's command to express His Majesty's appreciation of the loyal service given voluntarily to her country in a time of grievous danger by Dorothea Mary Plint as a Woman Home Guard Auxiliary.

The War Office, London.

Secretary of State for War

In the years when our Country was in mortal danger

SAMUEL ROWE.

who served from 20th.October 1943 to 31st.December 1944.

gave generously of his time and powers to make himself ready for her defence by force of arms and with his life if need be.

George R.I.

THE HOME GUARD

The certificates of service given at the end of the war to women auxiliaries and men in the Home Guard.

More than a million joined the Home Guard, which compared well with the Volunteer Force in November 1918 of 255,000. Many men in civil defence, fire service or police were spoken for. Yet the uncomfortable truth was that many men of the right age to join the Home Guard, chose not to.

People *not* doing something did not make a fuss or leave records, but the authorities felt their absence all the same. Salop district council in July in discussing the obstruction of landing places (in case of gliders), heard that one major had only five volunteers, including two boys, which was not enough to dig trenches. Brian Stewart joined the LDV in 1940 under age, while living in the village of Holyport near Maidenhead. His younger brothers thought it thrilling for Brian 'to go off to war'. His father who worked in the Stock Exchange, though a First World War Gallipoli veteran, did not join. 'I think he had enough in the First World War. He used to take me for walks on the Sunday. No, he didn't join us at all.'

Other veterans had had quite enough of fighting: Fred Barratt's father, for instance, who had been wounded in the chest and discharged. 'I tried to get him to join the Home Guard, but he didn't,' Fred recalled. Why not? 'I don't know; he didn't say much ... he didn't like hard work, Dad. He seldom spoke about the war.'

Even otherwise public-spirited men refused to serve. In Northampton, Peter Eads' father Frederick Charles was a regular soldier before 1914–18. He served

Rolleston and Stretton Home Guards near Derby on exercise, June 1941.

in France with the artillery, was wounded and later was an active member of the Old Contemptibles Association. Peter Eads remembered that

> He said he had no desire to play at soldiers in his Second World War. He still carried a big chip on his shoulder from 1918 when he and many others found themselves in the dole queue having been promised homes and jobs fit for heroes.

Perhaps some of the very old and disabled volunteered because they wanted to show they were as 'fit' as anyone else. On the Isle of Wight at Yarmouth, an ex-serviceman who had lost a leg in the last war insisted on having his name recorded. 'I should love to feel my cheek against the butt of a rifle again, having a pot at the blighters.' One police officer remarked that 'some of them were pretty old 65s' but they were all 'keen as mustard, and quite fit enough to shoot straight.'

In Lancashire, a man took his discharge papers from the last war to prove his war service, 'I hope this wooden leg of mine will not prevent my acceptance. I reckon I am still a good shot.' Reading between the lines, you sense that these amputees were seeking society's acceptance. How accepting had employers and women been to amputees in the previous twenty years?

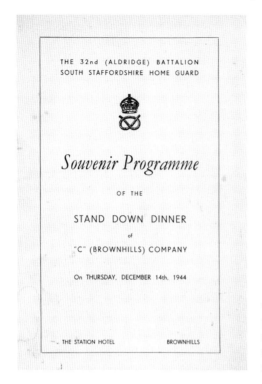

THE 32nd (ALDRIDGE) BATTALION
SOUTH STAFFORDSHIRE HOME GUARD

Souvenir Programme

OF THE

STAND DOWN DINNER

of

"C" (BROWNHILLS) COMPANY

On THURSDAY, DECEMBER 14th, 1944

THE STATION HOTEL   BROWNHILLS

The souvenir programme from a Staffordshire Home Guard company's stand-down dinner towards the end of the war. The anti-climax of the Home Guard's end obscured the very real need for it in 1940.

I offer you this quite inadequate little Souvenir, with my warmest thanks for your loyalty, keeness, efficiency and, above all, your friendship. Let us strive to keep alive the fine spirit of Service and Comradeship we have enjoyed together for over four years. Let us strive to do our bit for the future of the Homeland we were prepared to defend to the end.

Good Luck to you and yours!

T. J. H. HUME-HUMPHREYS,

Major,

O.C. "C" Coy. 32nd Bttn. South Staffordshire Home Guard

WHO WOULD HAVE WON?

Despite the Dunkirk evacuation and a string of defeats against the Germans in the next couple of years, many in Britain outwardly insisted that their Army was the best. Yet few Home Guards, then or ever, dared to claim they would beat a fully-armed, fully-trained invader. Bill Mycock in Monyash south of Buxton was, in old age, one of the more optimistic of the veterans of 1940.

The non-commissioned officers, and officers, were mainly men who had served in the First World War. They were trained soldiers, some had done four or five years in the forces so they were automatically given the ranks … I think we could have given as good as what we got because they were full of enthusiasm which counted for a lot. I mean it didn't bother us if it was pouring down with rain or thick fog, we just turned up.

Douglas Young in Hampshire said that 'We were reasonably effective, but wouldn't have been effective if a fully trained army had arrived, we would have been confined to sniping because there was no way there was enough of us to confront a large contingent of men.' The invading Germans might have run through England, despite hard resistance in some places, as the Allies did in Germany in April 1945.

HOW GOOD WERE THE HOME GUARDS?

Bernard Blake was born in Ashbourne in 1902, he went to Ashbourne Grammar School and so was as well educated as working people could be in those days. He began work as a Rolls-Royce apprentice, and became a motor mechanic. He knew his way around machinery and his locality – Blake arrived in Burton-on-Trent in 1927, at a garage at Derby Turn on the then main road from Burton to Derby. He would drive a repair truck when police called him to car accidents at night. His pages of notes and diagrams about lectures, kept by his son Don, a wartime schoolboy, suggest that the Home Guard was, for intelligent and practical men like Blake, something of an academy, and not only on military subjects. Don Blake's father joined in May 1940; 'He was devoted to it.'

Compare that with set-ups like the Nottingham unit that Robert Carver and his father belonged to. 'We wouldn't have stood a ghost of a chance,' was Robert Carver's view. Then a teenager, he recalls that he did not think about invasion, because he was

… more interested in cowboys and Indians … I remember the Saturday evenings were spent very largely playing cards, my Dad wouldn't let me play cards, but I used to stand and watch him; he used to win quite a lot at pontoon; then they would skive off to a local pub; I would be left standing at the door with my rifle and bayonet. You would do a little bit of a drill or you might do nothing at all and you were usually on duty until the morning so you would spend the night there and my Dad would see that I kipped down for the night; I don't know whether my Dad had any sleep or not, but he used to say go and get your head down, which I did. I had not quite two years of that.

Above: Jim Speed, Burton-on-Trent Home Guard private, signals unit.

Above right: A 1944 certificate of proficiency for young Burton-on-Trent Home Guard Ron Geary. In 1940 there was no form 'LDV 1'; incredibly, the nation's home defence effort began without any agreed weapons, uniforms, tactics or training.

Right: Guard Jack Rawlins in his back garden.

The truth, as ever, lies somewhere between the two extremes: in the experience of someone like Jack Rawlins. He went down the pit in Swadlincote, Derbyshire, then because of poor health he worked above ground, 'on the bank', as his nephew David Fleming recalled. Jack Rawlins would shoot rabbits in a farmer's field at the back of his house with his Home Guard rifle. David would be sent to collect the animal, in the hope that the farmer would overlook a child. Jack was a good enough shot to hit the rabbit in the head – a rifle bullet to the body would have exploded the creature, making it useless for the pot. In a family photograph Jack stands alone in uniform by the back garden shed. He looks awkward; it was odd for a man turned 50 to be dressed and equipped like a young man going to war. Such men seldom, if ever, fired a practice shot. Home Guard musketry was seldom of Army standard.

LIKE *DAD'S ARMY*?

'If you see the old *Dad's Army*, that's not unlike what it was,' said Douglas Young. Not all but some veterans of the Home Guard harked back to the 1970s BBC comedy series, such as John Henslow. In his published memoir – in 1940 he was at a Wiltshire private school – he recalled how on the Downs, he and fellow LDV men carried old single-fire Martini rifles from the Boys' Brigade, and five rounds

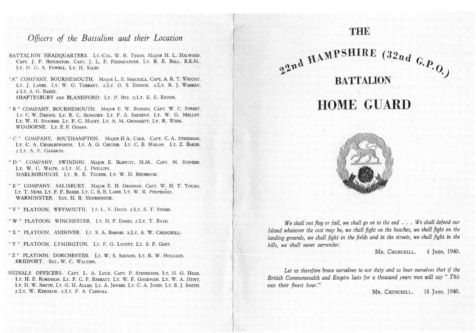

An end of service certificate for members of a Wiltshire and Hampshire Post Office battalion stressed Churchill's rousing speeches of June 1940. Did his line 'We shall never surrender' mean that Englishmen would fight the invader to the death?

of ammunition each. On the firing range they found that the rifles had no firing pins. Pull the trigger, and you merely heard a click.

Fred Barratt remembered that his unit commander 'was a bit of a snob … a bit of a Mainwaring'. Others, too, claimed to recognise the Walmington-on-Sea bank manager and Home Guard platoon commander. Robert Carver noted that 'We were very much left to our own devices, as long as chaps who had got the pips on their shoulders, that was perhaps really all they wanted. And be a Captain Mainwaring as it were.' Some, though, denied that the real thing was like *Dad's Army*, despite that programme's attention to detail and character. 'We were quite capable of fighting our way around, keeping under cover. We weren't a Dad's Army, I can assure you,' said Edward Yoxen, of Bedfordshire. Some could see both sides. 'So many people see *Dad's Army*, and they think that's what it was like,' said Fred Barratt. 'It was nothing like that. At times it was. But it was hard work.' The Bristol Home Guard A.J. Yeatman likewise called *Dad's Army* 'amazingly true to life', but feared it did the real guards 'a great disservice'.

A pencil drawing of Burton-on-Trent Home Guards leaving Waterloo Clump – a tower above the town – by torchlight. Absurdity and home defence were never far apart. 'Mind my stripe,' jokes the corporal. 'This way for the Elms,' the man in front says – the Elms being, of course, a pub.

HUMOUR

Dad's Army struck a chord because humour – as a way of releasing tension and passing the long nights in the guardroom – was never far away in 1940. Laughter could release fear. A laugh at yourself was the soul's defence against self-pity. A parade ground for a Home Guard company in Stoke-on-Trent was a cinder tip at the back of a gas works, 'where every shuffle of feet caused a cloud of dust serving as the prelude to a chorus of coughing'. The first issue of denim overalls as uniform could make you laugh or weep. One man in the Stoke railway Home Guard company demonstrated how his denims could be tied over his head with string, and the vent used 'for observation purposes'.

Did the humour show that deep down, some people did not take the threat of invasion seriously? Does this explain the range of responses in 1940, the shirkers and heroes, and the majority in between? To some people, an invasion was someone else's business. Dill wrote to Wavell on 6 June that 'The Government and all who matter here are in great heart and full of fight. *Most* people now know what they are up against and are determined to see this thing through.' [Author's italics.]

CHURCH COMPROMISE

Every person and every organisation had to ask themselves how far they would go to resist an enemy. Where it became interesting was when something cherished – which might be lost forever if an invader triumphed – came up against tradition that opposed any tampering, even if temporary and for the greater good. Take the use of churches for observation posts. Christians and the clergy were in a dilemma –

Chagford Church and Bovey Tracey Parish Church, Devon. The Church of England let Home Guards use towers as observation points but did not allow weapons – a sign of how the church could not reconcile its pacifist and nationalistic impulses.

what to render unto Caesar, and what to God? A July 'message to the nation' by the archbishops of Canterbury and York declared that 'The enemy is at the gate. A time of testing has come to this nation more severe and searching than ever before in the long story of its life.' How shall we meet the test, the leaders of the Church of England asked. Their answer seemed to be, leave it to others: 'We can rely on the wonderful unity of the people.' The archbishops also called for faith and prayer. At the other extreme, the Bishop of Hereford urged clergy to join civil defence, describing the war as 'truly a crusade'. He harked back to bishops of Hereford in the Middle Ages, guarding the Marches against invaders from Wales.

As for its towers, the Church of England negotiated a compromise – guards could go on watch, but not with any weapons or searchlights that might invite enemy attack. The churches sought to be a place to turn to 'in hour of need', but evidence as to whether church attendance increased is patchy.

DOUBTS AND INDIFFERENCE

Some had doubts. Jean Kershaw, who threw herself into the work, has lingering memories of people one could not trust if the enemy landed. As with so many in 1940 her life turned was upside down.

> I managed to resign from the Air Ministry joining Mum and Dad in Buxton where Dad's government office, the Customs and Excise, had been evacuated (to the Palace Hotel, if you know Buxton). I got a job as secretary to the town clerk – we were very busy with organising evacuees, blackouts, etc, I joined the WVS and worked two to three nights a week in the big services canteen we set up in the lovely Town Hall ballroom. All I seemed to do was pour hundreds of cups of tea and coffee and stir huge pans of baked beans each evening after work … One thing; we did not panic! … Meanwhile we all waited for 'the invasion'. I think most of us realised that we would have our backs to the wall … You really didn't know what was going on, I think we were all so tired, poor old mum was queuing for rations and veggies in the day and dad and I were out in the evenings.
>
> My dad [a veteran of 1914–18] talked quite seriously to Mum and I just once; after that, it [invasion] wasn't discussed. I think that it would have been a bloodbath had it happened – Brits don't give in easily. However, I'm sure and I do know from what was said by some, that there could have been a good few fifth columnists – you learnt to shun these folk. It made you realise what France, Holland, Belgium etc had gone through and you began to listen and 'suss out' who you could trust.

The suspicion is that some people did not do their fair share. They still took a holiday, or went on weekend-long cycle rides. By contrast, Edward Yoxen, in

1940 a 25-year-old draughtsman in a Bedford factory, rose through the ranks in the Home Guard. 'We just lived the war, really; you were at work or in the Home Guard, perhaps a bit of digging in the garden.' As Yoxen implied, men who put the hours in, in one part of their life, did so in others; even when they had time to themselves, they were doing something useful, such as growing vegetables for the table.

Frank Leatherdale was a rarity, a full-time member of the LDV in Leatherhead in Surrey, until he joined the RAF in November 1940 when he turned eighteen. He kept a note headed 'This is not an appeal for money – but for MEN' addressed to the people of Fetcham in Surrey, by the village's platoon commanding officer, W.H.G. Jenkins – 'to us he was Captain Jenkins'. He wrote: 'I feel quite certain that there are many eligible men still in the Parish who would be an asset to the Home Guard, and I appeal to them to come forward.' Such commanders would not waste their time with such an appeal unless they knew that some village men could join, but were choosing not to. 'The Fetcham platoon is doing all it can for you; see to it that you do all you can for it,' Jenkins concluded. But the first war had already shown that there are two sorts of people in the world; those that volunteer, and those that let them.

BAD HISTORY AND BAD VERSE

'Muddle through is almost a British virtue according to some people. It is not to me. It is a disgrace,' Labour minister Herbert Morrison told Durham Miners Hall on Saturday 20 June 1941. He and his audience were not to know that a few hours later the Germans would invade Russia, which for the time being saved England from invasion.

> We have stood behind our sea-girt walls for nine centuries always fighting our wars, except the civil wars, outside our country … Such a picture helps us to keep our nerves. This time last year it helped us to keep our nerves when every support on which we had counted was tumbling down around us.

He warned of the danger of thinking England could not lose – 'the country is still in danger.'

The Germans marched so far into Russia that any other country would have fallen. Geography mattered. What if the Channel had only been a few miles, like the narrowest water between Denmark and Sweden, not much more than the widest Russian river? Hitler would have been likelier, surely, to invade.

Morrison in any case was wrong. England had not stood unmolested behind sea walls 'for nine centuries'. The French landed in 1216; during the Hundred Years War; and on the Isle of Wight in 1545. The Spanish landed in the Cornish village of Mousehole and did as they pleased in 1596. Bonnie Prince Charlie sailed from France to Scotland to begin the '45; and the Dutch landed at Torbay and bloodlessly overthrew James II in 1688, although admittedly with the blessing of the English. England had a long history of feeling at risk from continental enemies – a list of invasion *scares* could be far longer.

A Rolleston and Stretton Home Guard commander, H.A. Parsons, testing his men in June 1941. The German invasion of Russia from that month removed the immediate risk of invasion.

The medieval walls of York, looking towards York Minster. These defences are a testament to England's long tradition of fearing – and repelling – invaders.

Two views of Lamorna Cove near Penzance in Cornwall. While some theorists like Basil Liddell Hart wondered if the Germans – like the Dutch in 1688 – would land first in the south-west, we now know that the Germans planned a more direct attack on the less rugged south-east.

A cause as good as the Home Guard had to inspire some bad but heartfelt poetry. From a Staffordshire man came a typed, undated poem entitled 'T'ome Guards' that imagined a conversation in the Reichstag (in Black Country accents?) between Goering, who wanted to invade Britain, and Hitler, who had doubts, for fear of the Home Guard. Goering told the Fuhrer

> Why ther only a Fred Karno army
> They only join up if they please
> They are bow legged an' knock-kneed and bandy
> wi' whiskers reight dahn ta ther knees.

Fred Karno, an Edwardian music-hall comedian, has faded from popular culture, unlike *Dad's Army*, and the names have the same shorthand meaning. 'Fred Karno's Army' meant clumsy, scruffy, disappointing to the proper military. Yet these men were ready to fight where they stood, even foolishly so. One wry story with wide currency in west Cumberland in July 1940, wide enough for the local weekly to print it, was that 'Parliament is to be petitioned to send the Regular Army to Egypt in order to give Hitler a fair crack of the whip against the LDVs over here.'

SOMETHING TO REPORT

At every turn there was more to 1940 than met the eye. Take the line 'nothing to report'. More than one Home Guard unit historian reflected on the irony that men might sing and swear, yet the only words in the guard book would be 'nothing to report'. A night's guard report in the City of London might have included 'the usual speculation of who put the last bullet in the ceiling. And Ginger the cat brings a dead rat to the sentry's feet.' Men snatched sleep on dirty blankets and perhaps endured an air raid alert for a couple of hours, but still the log would say 'nothing to report'.

Views of the fishing village of Mousehole near Penzance in Cornwall. Sacked by the Spanish in 1596, it was a reminder that England – far from being free of invasion since 1066 – in fact had a continual history of landings from the Continent.

The 'Spitfire summer' or 'invasion summer' of 1940, for all the sudden and shockingly unfamiliar threats to the homeland overall, was a skein of personal stories. A.E. Anslow, the platoon Home Guard sergeant in Seighford near Stafford, wrote in 1979, 'I can recall my own personal reaction when I was again dressed in the King's uniform. I felt a sense of pride in serving my country once more in a time of grave crisis.' He believed in persuasion of men, rather than coercion. 'That is the way I treated my men and today, years after the war, I am greeted with "good old sarge" by those with whom I had contact.' Anslow's experience was not all rosy; he could tell when he and his men were misused, like the time a drunk officer from RAF Seighford called out the platoon at midnight. While officers –military men with their career to make – passed through, the likes of Anslow tried to look after their men, who only wanted a quiet life at home.

The stories of frail and varied humans remain. In 2005, in the week he died, Kings Bromley man George Myatt recalled the Staffordshire village's Home

Above: Bunwell Home Guard unit in Norfolk, posing in front of Carleton Rode school.

Left: In front of a union flag and a portrait of the King and Queen, a Home Guard band at a dinner in early 1941 in Horninglow, Burton-on-Trent. Home defence turned out to be not all work.

Guard he saw as a boy. How a man stood in his community did not necessarily tally with his standing in home defence.

> Jack Billings was the sergeant; he didn't have a lot of respect in the village. As we grew up, we had a lot of respect for him; I think the people who had set him up as a cobbler were a bit disappointed [parish councillors, local farmers]. He had made a pig's ear of it. He had been in the first war; we always assumed he only had one leg. It was just one stiff knee. He used to ride a sit-up-and-beg bike; one leg doing all the work. He used to take the Home Guard sessions and you could detect his army background, or I could, as a kid. When he put on that uniform, he was a soldier, for an hour or two.

Workers at St Matthews Hospital in London asked Major K. Belsham to be their leader. He and other old soldiers at their local police station on the night of

Home Guard with a Vickers machine-gun on an unidentified village green in Surrey. (War Office official photograph by Len Puttnam.) Opposite, *Daily Mirror*, 26 April 1939; some pre-war bones of contention.

14 May 1940 were 'clamouring for rifles'. The police constable asked them: 'had we waited to hear the end of Mr Eden's broadcast? Rifles would appear in due course and not from the air or under the counter.' Irony and absurdity – and men with the ability to see it – were never far away in 1940. Belsham and the other men registered anyway, and planned the defence of their neighbourhood at the local British Legion headquarters.

'Invasion was a real danger, slowly receding but always present,' said the programme for the Buxton stand down parade in December 1944. Danger is something you cannot accurately measure. Was it all for nothing? Not according to Buxton.

> The constable, the sight of whom deters the criminal, is not less but more useful than he who arrests one after the crime has been committed. Only history will be able to estimate the influence which the Home Guard exercised upon the invasion plans of the common enemy.

History will not forget, so the programme said; but the last men of 1940 are passing away early in the twentieth-first century. A Home Guard unit historian from Surrey, R.A. Pepperall, tried to bridge the gap between earlier times and the unknown future: 'Readers who in 100, maybe 200 years time study a copy of this book in the library of the Imperial War Museum will find that we are in fact identical in essentials with the people who demanded their rights at Runnymede.'

Of all the moving words written about 1940, none are quite so touching as these. At war's end, the author was already writing of disappointment. To him it seemed inevitable that the men who stood their ground at Agincourt and defeated the Armada 'slipped back to domestic wrangles', as did the generation of 1940, who voted out Churchill in 1945. His men of 1940 were no better or worse than those before or since, because it was as he said: they were all the same people.

"DRAINPIPES"

"TERRIER," of West Hartlepool, Co. Durham, writes:—

No man would object to wearing his uniform off duty if it were smart.

But, in my opinion, British Army uniforms have become worse and worse.

Nothing could be more unattractive than the awful, knee - length "drainpipe" affairs we have to dress in.

Give us smartly-cut breeches to wear, like the Air Force and Artillery used to have, and see how many will be glad to appear off duty in "dress" uniform.

To-day's uniform certainly does not aid recruiting.

ANSWER: We should imagine that the breeches were done away with for some perfectly sound reason.

And though they might look smarter, we can't see a lot wrong with the lad in the picture.

No aid to recruiting?

Besides, "Terrier," the return of breeches would mean one more addition to a bloke's kit, all costing money.

Which may be all very fine for you moneyed elegants, but what about the ordinary bloke who just wants to join the Army, not a fashion parade?

ROYAL GREETING

Mr. E. H. FLOOD, of Rokeby-gardens, Woodford Green, Essex, writes:—

From many quarters I have heard expressions of disgust that the King should send congratulations to Hitler on his fiftieth birthday.

Both France and the U.S.A. rightly ignored a man who had so much innocent blood on his hands.

I am British and proud of it, but I feel a sense of shame that our name has been sullied by so many acts of bad statesmanship, of which this is the latest example.

ANSWER: And a lot more of our readers feel as you do, Mr. Flood.

Those responsible for advising his Majesty have once more shaken this country's faith by truckling to a man who understands nothing but force and merely sniggers up his sleeve at their tortuous political politenesses

D. W., of Bermondsey, S.E., writes:—

I am of the opinion that only men with money and a good education have any chance of becoming pilots in the R.A.F.

Am I wrong?

ANSWER: Completely.

But make sure you try to join for training AS a pilot.

PEOPLE'S CHOICE

Mr. D. STEEL, of Baldwyn Gardens, W.3, writes:—

Let the present Government allow the people to decide whether we have conscription or not.

Let everyone over the age of eighteen go to the Town Hall or other central place and vote whether such an Act should be put into force.

It means a lot of work for somebody, but it would keep the Government free from blame.

Mr. Steel.

ANSWER: And much more blame would break the Government's back, we should think.

Actually, we can't see much wrong with your idea, so long as it was left to the men to do the voting.

In fact, it'd be quite a change for the public to have a chance to say what it really does want, instead of having its elected leaders taking matters into their own gnarled, numb and fumbling hands.

"OLD 'UN" REPLIES!

Mr. DAVID MARKS, of Wenlock-road, N.1, writes:—

Now, about this young man of twenty-one who thinks th..t only the old 'uns should fight.

Did the young fellows of 1914 insist on the old men fighting for them?

Not on your life.

He says that the elderly ex - Serviceman knows all about war. Yes, but what did they know about it in 1914?

If he's too young to defend his country's interest at twenty-one, wasn't I rather young when I went to France to fight at the age of sixteen?

AND now you'll find me in the Territorials at the age of forty-one.

Mr. Marks.

ANSWER: No, Mr. Marks, we don't think the young man whose views set up an unpleasant smell on this page last week, would think you were too young. He'd just think you a sap.

He's probably quite prepared to be defended by sixteen-year-olds or sixty-year-olds. It's his own shrinking skin he's worried about

BIBLIOGRAPHY AND SOURCES

This book intentionally has no Spitfires or Hurricanes, nor Londoners under air raids. There are plenty of books on the Battle of Britain and the Blitz. Few books by comparison have covered the threat of German invasion. Even titles such as *Invasion Scare 1940* by Michael Glover (1990) turn out to be another re-telling of the Royal Air Force versus the Luftwaffe. It is hard to write about something that, after all, never happened. That has not stopped books being devoted to the supposed German landing in Suffolk, such as Peter Haining's *Where the Eagle Landed: The Mystery of the German Invasion of Britain, 1940* (2004). It is difficult to prove something did not happen.

Alternative histories are like chocolates – while you digest them they are enjoyable and you can believe they are even justifiable, but later you feel vaguely guilty for doing it. Alternative what-ifs include Kenneth Macksey's *Invasion: The Alternate History of the German Invasion of England, July 1940* (1999 new edition) and Martin Marix Evans' *Invasion! Operation Sealion 1940* (2004). Such books do raise profound questions. Is a past event pre-destined according to circumstance (in the case of the invasion, the state of the country, the military readiness of Germany), or could events have played out differently?

The Germans' plan for invasion – Operation Sealion – has not been analysed in this book partly because one of the truths of 1940 is that each side did not know what the other was doing. To keep the enemy guessing about your strengths and weaknesses was, and is, part of war. To give both sides of the 1940 story might give the wrong impression that everyone knew everyone's business. If they had, the Germans might have been keener to invade. As good a telling of the Sealion plan as any comes in the first couple of chapters of Chester Wilmot's *The Struggle for Europe*, still fresh, though published in 1952. Even earlier came his friend Basil Liddell Hart's *The Other Side of the Hill* (1948) that gave the war 'through German eyes', according to captured generals.

THE 13ᵀᴴ BN. NORTH STAFFORDSHIRE REGIMENT

HOME GUARD

NORTH STAFFORD

LDV

WE SHALL DEFEND OUR
ISLAND WHATEVER THE
COST MAY BE, WE SHALL
FIGHT ON THE BEACHES,
WE SHALL FIGHT ON THE
LANDING GROUNDS; WE
SHALL FIGHT IN THE FIELDS
AND IN THE STREETS;
WE SHALL FIGHT IN THE
HILLS; WE SHALL NEVER
SURRENDER.
(Winston Churchill, 4th June, 1940.)

1940

1944

TWO SHILLINGS & SIXPENCE

The cover of the Cannock Home Guard history. It contrasted the 1940 LDV – a miner in cloth cap and muffler – with the eventually far better equipped 1944 Home Guard.

Graham McCann sums up the Home Guard as well as anybody in his *Dad's Army: the story of a classic television show* (2001). Norman Longmate, a former Horsham Home Guard private who wrote *The Real Dad's Army* (1974) put 1940 into a larger context in *Island Fortress: the Defence of Great Britain 1603–1945* (1991).

Memoirs and diaries abound, touching on the possible invasion. These include *The London Observer, the Journal of General Raymond E. Lee 1940–1941* (1971), by the United States military attaché in London; *War Diaries 1939–1945, Field Marshal Lord Alanbrooke* (edited by Alex Danchev and Daniel Todman, 2001); *Peace and War, a Soldier's life*, by General Sir Frederick Morgan (1961), in summer 1940 defending his home county of Kent with the 1st Armoured Division; and *20th Century Journey: The Nightmare Years 1930–1940*, by William Shirer (1984).

Books published at the time have a poignancy, such as *A Prophet at Home* by Douglas Reed (1941), the journalist who sadly was already showing signs of the deluded conspiracy theorist he became. *The Lion and the Unicorn* (1941), though far from George Orwell's most famous work, and written arguably when his career was in a trough, shows him at his best.

The fiftieth anniversary of the war saw a burst of collections of reminiscences, including invasion: *Don't You Know there's a War on?* by Jonathan Croall (1989) – some of his witnesses accounts best taken with a pinch of salt – *Wartime Kent 1939–40* by Oonagh Hyndham (1990) and *Operation Cornwall* by Viv Acton and Derek Carter (1994).

The Mercian Maquis by Bernard Lowry and Mick Wilks (2002) covers the secret resistance organisation in Herefordshire and Worcestershire. See also the remarkable stories of teenage guerrillas in the *Lincolnshire Echo*, 1 October 1997.

No end of memoirs of famous people – from Denis Healey to Douglas Hurd – include 1940 in passing. The same goes for autobiographies of men who served towards the end of the war. These include *The Devil's Own Luck: Pegasus Bridge to the Baltic 1944–45* by Denis Richards (1999); *A Sapper in the Forgotten Army* by John Henslow (1986); *D-Day to Arnhem with Hertfordshire's Gunners* by Major Robert Kiln (1993), who defended beaches north of Newcastle; and *Accidental Warrior: In the front line from Normandy till Victory*, by Geoffrey Picot (1994).

Understandably, like Field Marshal Montgomery in his 1958 memoirs, all skate over 1940 compared with their harder fighting later. For a remarkably honest account of how an Army unit's junior officers in 1940 had to stick together faced with occasionally criminal common soldiers and bewildered commanders, see *Wars and Shadows: Memoirs of General Sir David Fraser* (2002), pages 137–9.

A tired-looking Ministry of Food Home Guard after an all-night exercise in 1942. When the ministry was evacuated to north Wales in 1940, even a letter to War Minister Eden by Food Minister Lord Woolton appealing for more rifles for his men was ignored.

Also worth browsing are old maps, such as the Ordnance Survey quarter-inch series (four miles to the inch, dated 1966). You get a feel for the 1940 landscape, of railway branch lines (since shut) and before bypasses or motorways. Sheet 17 of 17 covers south-east England, where any German invasion would have triumphed or failed.

Better still is to walk, to feel under your feet what the historian of *Dark Age Britain*, J.N.L. Myres, called the 'natural grain of the country' that an invader would follow. The Germans would have had eyes for river crossings and hilltops.

Even now you can view British defences such as pillboxes on the coast and inland. The only ready-made military monument at the National Memorial Arboretum in Staffordshire is a riverside pillbox, one of several on the west bank of that stretch of the River Trent. Tellingly, a sign – calling it a lookout post 'to be used in the event of Germany invading the south of England' – is inaccurate. You only have to look through the slit to realise it is about the worst possible lookout. It was there to shelter defenders against attackers from the east. If ever used, it would probably have been the site of the last stand of the British Empire.

SOURCES

Don't Panic is based on newspapers and documents of the time. As always, some local newspapers were more worth reading than others; most were useful for readers' letters, editors' comments, and court cases. Similarly, no two county record offices have the same holdings. Most have something about 1940 – whether Home Guard, police, civil defence or other local government records, or (as at Walsall) taped interviews or written memoirs and diaries. Dr Jack Longley's diary is in Bristol record office and Mrs Henry Dudeney's is in East Sussex archives at Lewes.

Added together the archives in the regions are an important, usually overlooked source. For one thing, they show that even parts well inland, hardly on the invaders' maps, took invasion seriously. The record office with the fullest Home Guard records, for instance, is in Northampton. The more that home defence developed and the more paperwork it generated, the weaker the threat of invasion became. Therefore holdings of Home Guard papers from 1940 are rare – the best are at Hampshire, Durham, and the London Metropolitan Archives (covering County Hall units). A less obvious but significant source are the police, who were used to paperwork; notable constabulary records covering 1940 are in Lincoln, Bristol and Cardiff.

The National Archives at Kew have central government and military unit records and Cabinet minutes. Many useful files are under HO 186 (Home Office) and WO 199 (War Office). Churchill making the defence of Whitehall his business: WO 199/617. About the Scilly Isles: WO 199/788. Australian soldiers on Salisbury Plain: WO 199/1616. The 1939 Army exercises: WO 199/1838. Evacuation of east

Some rather nervous-looking children present Australian soldiers with apples, southern England, October 1940.

and south-east coast towns: HO 186/349. For revealing private letters to Ismay, including Auchinleck's 'bollocks' comment: CAB 21/1158. For the RAF chewing over what to do in an invasion: AIR 2/7218; and the brave glider tests over the Channel: AIR 2/7225. For telling detail about one battalion – the 6th Durham Light Infantry – defending one piece of Dorset coast, see D/DLI 2/6/10 at Durham record office and WO 166/4220, National Archives.

Kew has many dozens of Home Guard unit histories, which vary from the short, staid and factual to the long, frank and funny. At the risk of showing Staffordshire bias, three favourites are of Cannock, Tettenhall and Aldridge. The Imperial War Museum at Lambeth, south London, also has many.

Dotted around libraries and record offices, and for sale second hand, are the many Home Guard manuals. Some in 1940 and after sold hundreds of thousands of copies. At first, the Local Defence Volunteers' and Home Guard's own official training instructions struggled to keep up. Full runs of those and related pamphlets are in the London Metropolitan Archives under HG. The unofficial 'how to' guides and the official instructions alike tell us about the weapons, training and tactics that the authors wanted to see – not necessarily the reality.

Horninglow, Burton upon Trent Home Guards at a dinner, February 1941. Invasion was less likely in the winter of 1940/1, but the question remained where and when Hitler would attack next.w

One theme has been how, faced with an outside threat, people show their true faces. So it was in Northern Ireland. For the 'remonstrance' that pointed out the Protestant-only home defence, see file HA/32/1/781 at the Public Record Office of Northern Ireland (PRONI).

Hours of handling old documents may leave your fingers black, but, at the National Archives especially, anyone can feel the awe of holding and reading a piece of paper signed by Montgomery or initialled by Winston Churchill.

Many men and women of the Home Guard, and their children, came forward in response to letters of mine in regional newspapers – such as the *Kidderminster Shuttle* for the 'Battle of Bewdley', and the *Eastern Daily Press* for the village of Carleton Rode. Particular thanks to the Liddell Hart Library at King's College London, which holds the Pownall diaries and many military history works; and Liddell Hart's newspaper cuttings. I have read newspapers and Home Guard histories in libraries around England and Wales – one fond memory is of a Cardiganshire battalion history one winter's night upstairs in Aberystwyth library.

INDEX